From Know-How
to Knowledge

From Know-How to Knowledge

The Essential Guide to Understanding and Implementing Knowledge Management

First published in 2000 by
The Industrial Society
Robert Hyde House
48 Bryanston Square
London W1H 7LN
Telephone: +44 (0)20 7479 2000

© Bryan Gladstone, 2000

© Typographical arrangement, The Industrial Society, 2000

ISBN 1 85835 880 9

Industrial Society
Business Books Network
163 Central Avenue
Suite 2
Hopkins Professional Building
Dover
NH 03820
USA

British Library Cataloguing-in-Publication Data.
A catalogue record for this book is available from the
British Library.

Library of Congress
Cataloguing-in-Publication
Data on File.

Printed by: J. W. Arrowsmith Ltd
Cover image by: Digital Vision
Cover design by: Sign Design
The Industrial Society is a Registered Charity No. 290003

Acknowledgements

This book would never have been written without the support and good wishes of some wonderful people.

My daughters Emily and Kate, who never doubted their dad's genius.

My Mum for her imagination, my Dad for his insight, and my brothers and sisters: all of them giving love and support.

My great friend and colleague, John Kawalek, who prompted me with his ideas throughout and helped me find the time to write.

David Megginson, a true friend and mentor.

John Blackwell, 'nuff said!

Geoff Smith, Business purpose, business purpose and business purpose!

The members of the Electronic Communication Forum for their ideas and stories.

The Birmingham Old Stars Basketball Club.

Susannah for her diligent editing and Carl for his patience and flexibility.

Friends and colleagues too numerous to name, but too valuable to neglect.

Last and most of all, my wife Mussart, who makes possible all my achievements!

I thank you all and absolve you from any blame for what follows. I may have laboured like an elephant, only to bring forth a mouse, but it's my mouse!

Foreword

Developing effective ways of managing knowledge is increasingly recognised as a key driver for exploiting latent corporate 'know-how' and offsetting competitive disadvantage. Knowledge management (KM) provides a horizon for organisations to think about their resident knowledge and to relate it to a wide range of business issues, such as the creation and retention of customers, the ability to apply corporate information to changing circumstances, the development and distribution of products and the prediction of future market behaviour and competitor strategies.

A new knowledge perspective is a requirement for competing in the twenty-first century. KM is becoming the next management paradigm, developing on from previous transformation strategies such as Total Quality Management, Business Process Re-engineering and Best Practices, and where solutions involve the integration of *people*, *processes* and *technology*.

To discuss key knowledge management concepts in an organisational context poses a difficult challenge. There is a great deal of hype and confusion about KM, as well as proprietary arrogance about the best solutions, and what knowledge issues (e.g. knowledge economy, management of intellectual capital, organisational design, knowledge and learning, corporate culture and KM strategy) need to be managed to make KM effective. There are many lessons being learned by early adopters, many experimenting with corporate intranets, 'communities of practice' or applying specific KM architectures, and a range of industries have already started to improve their understanding of knowledge and the way it is created, shared and applied in their business contexts.

From Know-How to Knowledge by Bryan Gladstone is a book for improving your understanding of knowledge and its relevance to organisations in the new millennium. It discusses key concepts in KM (e.g. information and knowledge relationships, the knowledge process, managing knowledge resources and the limitations of so-called 'knowledge management solutions'), and introduces the idea of the 'virtual shop floor' as the conduit which intuitively exploits the information, knowledge and processes which make businesses a reality.

Backed-up by high level corporate interviews and extensive research, *From Know-How to Knowledge* also provides useful case studies to stimulate creative thinking about 'knowledge', as a prelude to context-based knowledge management action.

Dr. Allan Taylor
Senior Lecturer in KM, University of Abertay, Dundee, and
Senior Consultant HD Management, Edinburgh

Contents

1. What is knowledge management? 1

2. Better information management is not enough 23

3. The knowledge creation cycle 47

4. Why knowledge management now? 71

5. What knowledge needs managing? 87

6. The processes of knowledge management 105

7. Being a knowledge manager 123

8. Conclusions – the future of knowledge management 145

Further reading 153

Introduction

'Here is Edward Bear, coming down stairs now, bump, bump, bump, on the back of his head, behind Christopher Robin. It is, as far as he knows, the only way of coming down stairs, but sometimes he feels that there really is another way, if only he could stop bumping for a moment and think of it.'

A. A. MILNE, WINNIE-THE–POOH, 1926

Why knowledge management?

Sometime during the 1990's a line was crossed. Before then, in most industries, in most markets and in most jobs, it was enough to know how to perform more efficiently than the competition. Industries, markets and jobs had boundaries, technologies and purposes, the stability of which could be trusted.

Know-how, the capacity to do *a particular thing*, remains the key to personal and corporate success, because we do those particular things to satisfy our own and our customers' particular needs. But the world has changed – the knowledge era has arrived.

There is no simple way to describe the knowledge era. Its main characteristic is that the *particular things* that markets demand are changing faster and faster. Today's markets, today's standards, today's leading edges, these have become fickle and untrustworthy bases for long term success.

In the knowledge era, stable environments have given way to rapidly shifting ones that can make highly valued skills and knowledge worthless overnight. Managers need to keep checking that their trusted solutions are still relevant. In most industries, yesterday's know-how is now history, and we can be fairly confident that today's will soon be just as out-of-date.

It is not the end of know-how, but it is the end of thinking of it as enough to support the survival of the business. In the knowledge era, the particular things are still the golden eggs of our knowledge processes. They are what deliver success to organisations *on the day*, but it is our knowledge processes that lay those golden eggs. We should value the eggs we have got, but we had better take awfully good care of that goose if we want more eggs in future.

It is the pace and nature of change that is driving the establishment of knowledge management. This is hardly the first era in which successful corporations have lost their leading positions, but what is new is their number and the pace. Satisfied with where they already are, such organisations risk ending up like Digital, unable to make the shift from selling mini-computers in a world that wants personal computers, or like practically all Britain's high street banks, losing market share to on-line bank First Direct and its followers, because they wanted to stay banks when their market wanted retailed financial services. A decade ago Japanese corporations dominated world markets completely with their exceptional capacity to deliver quality. Today, they are just other competitors.

Know-how only has value as long as the market values the '*how*'. When I was growing up in Illinois in the 1960's, my parents traded stocks and shares through their broker in Chicago, who traded on the floor of the stock exchange. Today, I buy and sell my own shares through the Internet. More significantly, it is not just penny traders like me, but massive institutional investors who are doing their own stock broking. The traditionally exclusive and valuable skill of trading shares has become common knowledge and its commercial value has plummeted. Knowing how is not enough when the market decides to use a different channel or to buy a different product.

The line was crossed when the unknown competitors and the unknown technologies became more important than the known, when expertise and knowledge advantage became perishable commodities that had to be exploited fully now, because the only certainty was that they would not last. Today's know-how is as perishable as today's newspaper. Try selling *that* next week and see how many customers you get.

What is knowledge management?

The very thought of managing knowledge makes some people uncomfortable. For a start, what do we mean by it? One way to introduce knowledge management to groups is to ask them to define the words *'knowledge'*, *'information'* and *'data'* without using those words or their derivatives such as *'know'* or *'inform.'* The variety of definitions is only limited by the number of people present. You cannot hope to be a knowledge manager without understanding the importance of your own and your organisation's definitions.

Knowledge management is not about knowledge so much as the capacity to know. To manage knowledge is to concentrate on supporting its processes to achieve business objectives. It represents a fundamental step away from the management of things towards a concern for ideas. These are the issues that knowledge management addresses:

- Where does our know-how come from?
- How can our know-how be identified and shared better in our organisation?
- What know-how will our organisation need tomorrow?
- How can we improve organisational capacity to learn and share tomorrow's know-how?
- How can we improve our capacity to put aside know-how that is no longer helpful?

In part, the need for knowledge management lies in the rise of information and communication technology – the way it has turned information into a common good. The days when the mere possession of information conferred a killing advantage are long gone. Anyone can search the Web, and everyone does. Managers who *'stick to the knitting'* are risking everything, because the world is changing fast. Their customers and competitors are in touch with each other. Next year's eBays, Amazon.coms and Gateways are already taking shape in someone's garage or back room.

Who should read this book

This is not a recipe book of the sort that proliferates on management bookshelves – it will not tell you exactly *what* to do, because the recipe that will work in your organisation will be unique to it. If it were that easy, why is it that so many successful CEO's are unable to repeat their successes when they move on?

Its purpose is to introduce the key concepts of knowledge management and to describe some of the approaches taken by organisations which manage their knowledge and knowledge processes. Some tools described here may work in your organisation, but it would be foolish to see them as recipes for you to follow. *From Know-How to Knowledge* is written for readers who want to understand the tool, knowledge management, and not just to apply it in ignorance of its basic principles.

There are managers in organisations where knowledge management is being introduced who need to understand it in order to participate in an informed way and to help their teams accept it. More than that, every manager has already, or will soon, come into contact with customers, suppliers and competitors who are managing knowledge. This book will give them a basis for making sense of it and responding intelligently.

The need to manage knowledge

- According to the Malcolm Balbridge Foundation, 88% of Fortune 1000 company CEO's consider improving knowledge management to be a critical business issue, but only 23% rate themselves as truly capable knowledge managers.
- According to the Delphi Group, over 90% of the Fortune 1000 corporations already invest or propose to invest in knowledge management within the next four years.
- Corporate spending on knowledge management software is predicted to rise to $25 billion by 2003.
- IBM has cut its own spending on information technology by over 30% since 1993 through knowledge management. During the same period, its hardware product to market time has fallen from a mean average of four years to sixteen months. More than half its products are market-ready in less than six months.

IBM Corporation, 1999

You do not need to be an information technologist to read *From Know-How to Knowledge*. In fact, if you believe that knowledge management is just another IT application, it will disappoint you. Knowledge management uses information technology, but its primary focus is on people. They are the ultimate source of corporate success, because they are the source of knowledge. *From Know-How to Knowledge* will give you the understanding and practical insights that you need to start on the journey, but it is your journey.

The structure of the book

The book is divided into eight chapters that set out the core concepts and introduce key practices in knowledge management. In **chapter one**, we consider what knowledge management is by introducing the concepts of the *real* and the *virtual shop floors*. The real shop floor is much more than just the production area in a factory. It is used in this book to represent all the visible things that people do in organisations – tele-workers make phone calls, sales people make customer calls, architects draw plans, construction workers build houses. The real shop floor is the traditional realm of management. It is real because we can observe what happens on it. It is the realm of explicit, measurable things such as hours worked, production levels and productivity. Organisations need to perform well on the real shop floor, because that is where profits are generated. The real shop floor is a metaphor for where things get done.

Behind the measurable and measured real shop floor there is a hidden virtual 'place' where organisational knowledge is created, shared and used. The virtual shop floor is where people's minds meet. It is altogether more problematic, because it is not a visibly 'real' place. The virtual shop floor only exists because of the *'real'* things that people do in organisations, but the real shop floor is just as dependent on the knowledge work of the virtual shop floor. Managers are, understandably, happiest with processes that they can see, and that produce predictable outputs. The problem with knowledge creation is that its processes are a mystery and there is no guarantee that they will produce desired results.

Chapter two examines the role and limitations of information. The terms 'knowledge work' and 'knowledge worker' are used to place information in context. Knowledge work is, simply, the process of learning, sharing and creating that accompanies the doing of tasks by individuals and teams. One of the outputs of knowledge work is information. The less routine the task, the more intensive and important the knowledge work is likely to be. The driving force behind the rise of information management has been the notion that systems can enable competitive advantage in the comprehensiveness, quality and distribution of information. Highly functional information systems have been created, but have they brought returns that justified their cost? The problem is that information does not have value in itself. Where the archaeologist stumbles across the remains of a lost civilisation, most of us only stub our toes!

In business we tend to equate the possession of information with being able to use it. Yet a moment's thought reveals the absurdity of such a view. Half the fun in reading Arthur Conan Doyle is in contrasting Dr. Watson's plodding with Sherlock Holmes' analytical brilliance. It is only *'elementary, my dear Watson,'* to those whose knowledge processes are up to the job. There is never a shortage of information in a Sherlock Holmes mystery – it is just that no one but Holmes is clever enough to make sense of it all. Corporations cannot go on improving their information systems if, Dr. Watson-like, their information strategies are somehow disconnected from corporate knowledge processes.

Chapter three goes deeper into the relationship between information and knowledge. It explores how knowledge is created and considers how knowledge work has been overlooked because of the way that it can be hidden behind more visible and manageable *'doing'* activities. A model is introduced to explain the relationship between knowledge processes and information and to make clear why information is only valuable if there is knowledge, and purpose to give it meaning.

Information collected for its own sake swiftly clogs up systems. Information management adds value when the system supports and encourages the flow of the information that knowledge workers need and use and discourages the flow of information that they do not need and use. Thus knowledge management is primarily the management of the processes that generate knowledge, rather than the management of knowledge itself.

The management challenge of knowledge processes is to make organisations better at learning, creating and sharing. It requires an understanding of how the virtual shop floor operates in order to improve its efficiency and effectiveness in support of organisational objectives.

When employees feel unable to share lessons that they have learned, when opportunities to innovate are consistently missed, or when people are regularly unable to collaborate in ways that could benefit the organisation, then these are failures of process that effective management ought to be able to prevent.

Chapter four is concerned with why knowledge management is an issue now, when it was not previously. It considers why and how the business environment is becoming increasingly competitive. Corporations are managing knowledge because they have to. To fail to do so is to leave an opening for others. The possibilities knowledge management offers are made necessities by the forces of competition. Corporate success comes from identifying strategic priorities and mobilising resources to concentrate on those priorities. If knowledge really is the vital resource, then it must be managed to maximise its efficiency and effectiveness in the service of the organisation.

The focus of **chapter five** is on what aspects of knowledge should be managed. The contradictory demands of efficient real shop floor performance and organisational capacity for effective change are explored.

Knowledge serves two primary functions within organisations. First, knowledge enables organisations to cope with an uncertain future. This involves recognising trends and opportunities, predicting coming events and, in general, making sense of the unfamiliar. Organisations are better able to cope when managers can picture possible future scenarios and so be prepared for, and possibly use, any situation to advantage. Thus, one of the key effects of knowledge management is to motivate organisation members by helping ensure that the organisation is not surprised by the unexpected.

The second purpose is to enable the efficient operation of the real shop floor. The development and sharing of practices and processes to achieve improved productivity has been a primary aim of management throughout the last century. While the two purposes are complementary, it may be the case that efficiency is pursued at the expense of effectiveness.

Chapter six concentrates on the practical challenges of managing knowledge. It builds on principles introduced in earlier chapters. There are standard knowledge management tools and processes, but how they are developed and used will be different in each organisation. Knowledge management systems cannot be slavishly copied from 'first in the field' leaders or taken off the shelf and applied willy-nilly.

For business tools to work they must be applied in a manner that is sensitive to the way the affected people think and behave. Approaches are described in this chapter which have achieved spectacular successes, and failures. Which result depends on how well managers understand their purposes in introducing it and the processes of their own virtual shop floors.

Chapter seven discusses what the practice of knowledge management actually means to managers. Like any other management focus, it has its objectives, means and metrics.

It is important to start with the recognition that all managers manage knowledge, whether they mean to or not. Everyone participates as fully on the virtual shop floor as they do on the real one. Decisions to limit coffee breaks, close the smoking room or do anything else that affects communication, learning and doing are knowledge management decisions as much as operational management ones.

Every organisation interacts with its environment differently, but the principles of knowledge management still apply. Above all, knowledge management depends on an appreciation of organisational objectives. The very complexity, expense and promise of the technologies of information management and communication have made it easy to overlook why they have become central to organisations so quickly and completely. They offer the prospect of achieving corporate purposes more effectively by facilitating knowledge processes. Once managers can place corporate knowledge processes within a strategic framework, defining practices and applying metrics becomes possible. Just as vaguely focused quality initiatives were utterly transcended by tightly defined and measured Total Quality Management, so the fuzzy and uncertain visions of knowledge-based, information-rich organisations will be left behind as genuine applications of knowledge management prove their worth.

Crossing the line

One of the more comic over-assertions about knowledge management is that organisations that do not manage knowledge formally do not develop or apply knowledge. That is absurd. As well to say that no one manages anything unless they have 'manager' in their job title. As a young economist, I was made to appear rather foolish in a candidates' discussion when I wisely observed that the government had no local taxation policy. The candidate who got the job trumped me with a pitying, '*Not having a policy is a policy by default.*' He was right, of course.

As with taxation policy, so with knowledge management. All corporations develop, collect, filter, save, distribute and apply knowledge. They influence knowledge processes, whether they call it knowledge management, information management, administration or tap-dancing. So this book is not about organisations doing something new, but about understanding what they already do by default and considering how it might be done better.

Our knowledge is what defines who we are. It is the source of our self-respect and economic well-being. As you read this book, employees around the world will be creating, sharing and applying knowledge for themselves and for their organisations. They always have done. You are doing it now, as you read. Even if none of the intended messages gets through to you, your knowledge has been altered.

Knowledge management is about harnessing and supporting these knowledge processes. It is being done intentionally and effectively in more and more organisations around the world. The line has been crossed by too many managers and too many corporations to turn back now. The knowledge era has arrived. Know-how is not enough any more.

1

What is knowledge management?

Introduction

Knowledge management is here, but what is it? Haven't we got enough to do without another new craze? In the past twenty years we have been down-sized, de-layered, refocused, restructured and process re-engineered. We have poked and prodded our organisations into cycles of endless change in pursuit of better performance. Our quality became total, our change became continuous and our teams became virtual, all to cope with a world business environment that got smaller, turbulent, complex and globalised. Do the groaning shelves of the airport bookstores really need another new business fad?

Well, yes, I am afraid they do. After two decades working with electronic information and communications technologies, managers are recognising that success is not about getting people to work with IT, but about helping people to work with other people. Knowledge management is explicitly about how people learn and share together in organisations. As such it is the only way to ensure that all our expensive investments in information handling and communications actually prove worthwhile.

'Knowledge work' needs knowledge management

'The fact is, more and more jobs – no matter what the title – are taking on the contours of "knowledge work." People at all levels of the organisation must combine the mastery of some highly specialised technical expertise with the ability to work effectively in teams, form productive relationships with clients and customers and critically reflect on and then change their organisational practices. And the nuts and bolts of management – whether of high-powered consultants or factory technicians – increasingly consist of guiding and integrating the autonomous but interconnected work of highly skilled people.'

Chris Argyris, 'Teaching smart people how to learn', *Harvard Business Review*, May-June 1991

Without knowledge management, our systems may end up like the priceless Lamborghini roadster in the farmer's barn. *'You mean, it's been serving as a chicken coop?'* shrieks the vintage car collector, as he views its rusting hulk. *'Yep,'* says the farmer, *'and a darned good one, too.'* Research suggests that more than 65% of information technology investments are judged to have failed, even when the people who are supposed to use it are included in the design of the systems[1]. They may not all be serving as chicken coops, but nor are they taking their owners for luxury rides down the information super-highway. It is not that the technology does not work: it usually does. It's just that the organisation does not benefit from it enough to justify the high investment costs.

---

[1] Deborah Howcroft and Melanie Wilson, 'Paradoxes of participatory design: the end-user perspective.' Paper given to the International Critical Management Conference, Manchester Business School, 7–9 July 1999.

The virtual shop floor – where people's minds meet

Knowledge management is not about setting up a new department, as you sometimes find with smaller firms where marketing, say, or human resource management has simply been neglected as the firm grew. It is about recognising that knowledge generation, sharing and application are the most important activities of nearly every person in every department in every organisation. To understand that fact is to reconsider the way organisations operate. There is a real shop floor that is visible and a virtual shop floor that is hidden.

The real shop floor is the traditional realm of management. It is real because we can see it, and see what happens on it. It is the realm of explicit measurable things. *'Don't bring me problems. Bring me solutions!'* cries the hyper-busy real shop floor manager. He wants that report on his desk by lunch time. That order had better be shipped by Friday, and no excuses! Organisations need to perform well on the real shop floor, because that is where profits are generated. The real shop floor is a metaphor for where things get done by organisations.

At a typical English village pub in Warwickshire, the White Swan, the landlord, Billy, takes stock, knows all the costs and prices of drinks, opens for a set period every day, monitors the hours and activities of bar staff and keeps accurate accounts. When a barrel of beer cracked in his cellar during a delivery, he bought a new loading mat. When a barman is late, he can have a word with him or dock his pay. He plans the restaurant menu and keeps financial records. All these things contribute to how well the pub is performing as a profit centre.

The virtual shop floor is where people's minds meet. It is an altogether more problematic concept. Behind the measurable and measured real shop floor there is a hidden virtual 'place' where organisational knowledge is created, shared and used. At the White Swan, for instance, knowing the quirks of different customers is essential to keeping them happy. Billy reckons it took him three years to develop the right 'atmosphere,' but he can only describe what he means in the vaguest of terms. He just '*knows*' that the success of the White Swan depends on it.

Everywhere there is a real shop floor, there is a virtual one too. The virtual shop floor only exists because of the '*real*' things that people do in organisations, but the real shop floor, where we do things, is utterly dependent on the knowledge work of the virtual shop floor. The task-focused real shop floor manager may be too busy to be concerned about why and how solutions are reached, but in every organisation people work these things out on the virtual shop floor.

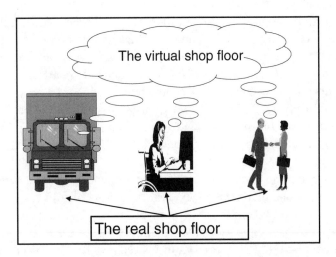

The real shop floor – where things are done

Picture the real shop floor. It is much more than the production area of a factory. It is everywhere that employees perform the actions required to accomplish organisational tasks and processes – the telesales person makes a call, the carpenter hammers in a nail, the surgeon sets a broken leg. Communications are routine, factual and formal: what appointments have been booked for Tuesday? How many cars rolled off the assembly line last month? Its tools are the calculators, chainsaws, photocopiers, frying pans and lathes that employees use to turn inputs into outputs. Its processes are physical, repetitive and linear. It is *real* in the sense that the activities on it can be seen, counted, costed and valued. The real shop floor is where things are done and is the traditional realm of management. Above all, its activities are visible.

The two names most often associated with the workings of 'the real shop floor' are those of Frederick Taylor and Henry Ford. Taylor developed the notion of Scientific Management. This involved identifying the most efficient possible means of completing tasks and, then, organising production systems so that all workers performed tasks in the same, most efficient, manner. Henry Ford developed his own version of Taylorism as an industrial philosophy and, in so doing, lay down the foundations of business and management in the twentieth century. Ford and Taylor shared a belief in the need to see and control the activities of operatives in ways that benefited the organisation.

All the significant actions and outputs of the real shop floor can be observed, counted and valued by time-and-motion specialists like Frederick Taylor or through financial and other records. We can know, for instance, exactly how many miles a salesperson drove, the number of calls made and the total sales achieved. School managers track photocopier use by academic subject group and could track photocopying of individual lecturers if they wanted. In telephone call centres, the calls of operatives are monitored to find out how many leading questions they ask and how many closing statements they make.

The vitual shop floor

The virtual shop floor refers to the metaphorical 'place' where learning, creating and sharing of knowledge happens. Before modern communications, the virtual shop floor would have occurred in, essentially, the same physical environment as the real shop floor because people would communicate mainly with others who were in the same location. The opportunities to communicate more widely were limited. Today's information and communication networks, however, have spread the virtual shop floor. Consultants working for Buckman Laboratories in Capetown can call on advice from colleagues from around the world at a moment's notice. When a BP-Amoco oil rig in the North Sea develops a problem, engineers in Texas and Singapore might be able to help.

The virtual shop floor's function is to develop and spread knowledge and information. There is no individual like Frederick Taylor or Henry Ford associated with 'the virtual shop floor', but a large number of people and organisations have contributed to its exploration. Several deserve a mention:

- Marshall McLuhan, the Canadian philosopher of mass media and popular culture, pointed out in the 1950's and 1960's that the way societies communicate is more important than what they communicate. He coined the phrase, '*The medium is the message*,' and was the earliest writer to recognise how electronic communications would free many workers from '*the tyranny of place*.' He called such workers '*nomads of knowledge*' and warned that corporations would come to need them more than they needed corporations in his 1964 classic *Understanding Media*[2].

- Ikujira Nonaka is widely credited with establishing knowledge management as a legitimate subject. He wrote a seminal article on the 'knowledge creating company' in 1991[3]. His key contribution was to argue convincingly how important knowledge-creating activity is to company performance even when such activity does not contribute to corporate efficiency in the short or medium term. In one of his cases he describes how a researcher at Matsushita apprenticed herself to a master bread maker for a year in order to learn skills that she later mimicked to design Matsushita's market-dominating automatic home bread-maker.

---

[2] Marshall McLuhan, *Understanding Media*, Signet, New York, 1964.

[3] Nonaka Ikujira, 'The knowledge creating company', *Harvard Business Review*, November–December 1991.

● A number of different people, including American academic authors Chris Argyris and Peter Senge, helped popularise the concept of corporations as organisations whose success depended on their capacity to learn. Argyris' concept of double-loop learning is particularly important because of the way it throws attention on the different types of learning that are possible. In particular he introduced the metaphor of double-loop learning. The single-loop is learning what or how to do something. The double-loop occurs when learners reflect on the reasons why things are done. One of his most appropriate lessons for knowledge managers is that managers are often the worst learners[4]:

'… because many professionals are almost always successful at what they do, they rarely experience failure. And because they have rarely failed, they have never learned how to learn from failure. So, whenever their single-loop learning strategies go wrong, they become defensive, screen out criticisms and put the "blame" on anyone and everyone but themselves.'

Single-loop and double-loop learning

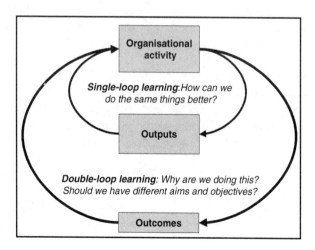

---

[4] Chris Argyris, 'Teaching smart people how to learn', *Harvard Business Review,* May–June 1991.

Many managers, who are unwilling or unable to engage in double-loop learning, may be tempted to focus narrowly on managing knowledge about how to improve organisational capacities to produce outputs. Their responses reflect the difficulty involved in reviewing and questioning the wisdom of previous decisions. It is hard to change direction when it may mean abandoning positions that have brought personal and corporate success in the past.

● Arie de Geus has both explored the concepts of the learning organisation in his writings and applied them while a senior executive at Shell[5]. In particular, de Geus has argued that:

'With capital easily available, the critical production factor shifted to people. But it did not shift to labour. Instead, knowledge displaced capital as the scarcest production factor – the key to corporate success.'

Comparing real and virtual environments

The effect of these developments has been to force managerial attention towards the virtual shop floor, a place so unfamiliar that some consultants have urged managers to put on their pith helmets and go exploring. Here is Victoria Ward, the former Chief Knowledge Officer at NatWest Markets[6]:

'Systematic mapping of the location of knowledge and information assets needs to take place in conjunction with the creation and formalisation of communities of navigators, or local guides, who act as collaborators in the creation, distribution and development of the map, and in the location, guardianship and development of valuable knowledge assets.'

The notion of a map brings to mind strange and unknown places, but the virtual shop floor need not be so alien. Organisations all generate knowledge, so it is where we operate. Organisations hum with mental activity, even if we do not manage it as well as we

---

[5] A. De Geus, *The Living Company*, Nicholas Brealey, London, 1997.

[6] Victoria Ward, 'Mapping meta knowledge – a cartographic approach', *Knowledge Management Review*, Issue 5, November/December 1998.

could. Consider and compare the characteristics of the virtual and real shop floors:

Place: The real shop floor means more than the production area of a factory. It includes all the places where employees operate. It is visible to managers. It houses the capital equipment that workers use and is where materials are brought to be changed into outputs. In the case described overleaf, it was the office where consultant John McRobie was expected to write out his reports. Managers can monitor what people are doing on the real shop floor. Even when employees are physically separated by distance, their real performance can be monitored in the form of sales figures, jobs signed off and so on.

The virtual shop floor is a hypothetical 'place' where learning, creating and sharing of knowledge happen. Before modern communications, the virtual shop floor would have occurred in, essentially, the same physical location as the real shop floor because people would communicate mainly with others in the same physical location. An apprentice, for instance, would learn while working alongside a master craftsman. With the advent of the telephone, e-mail, video-conferencing and the Internet, however, the notion of physical place has melted away. Teams can collaborate and communicate across continents as readily as across corridors. When a problem occurs on a North Sea oil rig, engineers gather from around the world in a matter of hours via video link. Ten years ago they would have had to fly to Scotland.

Participation: While activities on the real shop floor are easy to observe, count, cost and value, virtual participation is much more problematic. Its key is communication, which can occur in so many ways that it may not even be clear who is participating. The appearance of deep thought, for example, may be a mask for day-dreaming. Sometimes, as in the case overleaf, managers may interfere with highly productive virtual shop floor participation in their efforts to enforce visible real shop floor participation.

Not a team player...

One of the cleverest social and economic consultants in England is John McRobie. Before he set up on his own he endured several years of mistrust in a consultancy firm where they needed his expertise but hated the way that he preferred to think about difficult issues and write up reports at home. He was always available to help other consultants at the office or over the phone, but when deadlines were tight and the problem was thorny, he preferred to work in his own study. Despite John's record as a contract winner and client pleaser, all knew that his future was not with the firm. Against the evidence of his clients' views and the arguments of his colleagues, the MD and the CEO were agreed. He was *'not a team player.'* In the end, he left to set up on his own.

Ironically, his first big projects as an independent were with his ex-employers. They still needed to employ his knowledge capacities. Once he was an outside consultant contracted to deliver outputs, the problem of his preferred working style ceased to be an issue. His 'unmanageability' was no longer a management concern.

The term *communities of practice* has been coined to describe one of the most important aspects of participation on the virtual shop floor. Communities of practice are sets of people who share a professional interest and band together to share their knowledge and learn from each other. Such communities draw members from different physical locations, different levels of seniority and even from different organisations who may stay in contact through information technology, regular meetings or through casual chats. Jerry Hirshberg, who set up Nissan Design International, pointed out the dangers of designating some people as creative and others as not when he described how the contribution of a secretary, Mrs Woo, dramatically improved a prize-winning automobile design[7].

'The potential for some level of creativity exists in everyone. Contrary to popular myth, original thought is not restricted to rare individuals in isolation. It is a uniquely human enterprise that requires critics and supporters, senders and receivers, real-world grounding and unrestricted flights of imagination. While some are clearly more predisposed than others, without a fundamental grasp of the pains and joys of birthing ideas there would be no place for them to grow or be realised. By exposing and involving people such as Mrs Woo in parts of the creative process we have found a heightened capacity for timely and incisive observations along with greater receptivity and supportiveness for new, often uncomfortable, concepts when they appear.'

Communication: On the real shop floor, the limits of communication are clearly defined by the industrial process. Salespersons communicate with account managers, dispatchers and other salespersons. Operatives on an assembly line communicate with the people they work alongside. The industrial process requires communication, but makes it relatively easy for managers to control it. At its most extreme, no talk at all is allowed on some real factory shop floors. Huw Beynon quotes a worker for Ford before the Second World War[8].

'Those of us who worked in the Dagenham plant... recall the fear of talking out of turn... The Gestapo-like Service men, and the cat-walk high above the factory where the superintendent patrolled for all the world like a prison warder, shouting down to any unfortunate who happened to have a word with a fellow worker...'

More than sixty years later, Simon Caulkin of *The Observer* was comparing conditions in British callcentres to Victorian sweatshops[9], *'Conditions at Britain's 4,000 callcentres often resemble factory farms rather than twentieth-century offices.'*

---

[7] Jerry Hirshberg, *The Creative Priority*, Harper Perennial, New York, 1998.

[8] Huw Beynon, *Working for Ford* , 2nd ed, Pelican, London, 1984.

[9] Simon Caulkin, 'Sweatshops – the wrong call', *The Observer*, 28 November 1999.

The starting point of such an approach is denial of the potential value of the virtual shop floor. The virtual shop floor, though, is entirely dependent on communication. People communicate with whoever seems appropriate in order to generate and share knowledge. There are many ways to communicate and, thanks to modern communications technology, a vast number of people to communicate with.

In the story below Jim communicates widely so he is better prepared to deal with customer problems, but it would probably come as a shock to his managers if they realised how much he depends on people who are not always fellow employees. He is both improving his real shop floor contribution and breaching a corporate fire wall. Yet management is only aware of what he is doing on the real shop floor and does not understand how or why.

A view from the virtual shop floor

Jim is a senior technologist in a blue chip company who was asked to describe his community of practice. His interview demonstrates how employees participate on the virtual shop floor whether or not it is formally managed.

Q.   How well does the Internet work for you?

Jim: *'It's very good. I have used it for five years. I know many people around the world who can help me.'*

Q.   How do people around the world help you?

Jim. *'[We] talk by e-mail, Internet relay chat, personally too… sometimes at cybernetic meetings. … When I started using the Internet I learned many things from a 14 year-old kid on the other side of the world.'*

Jim's primary motivation in work is to do his job better. He looks to his community to help him perform better on the real shop floor. *'The worst thing that can happen is that I go to a client and I can't resolve the problem. I try to avoid it happening.'*

An illustration of how communication can be supported by knowledge management comes from Xerox. In its Eureka Programme it has linked its service engineers, so that repair problems and solutions throughout the world can be shared within the wider community of Xerox service engineers. Expertise is transferred and its impact magnified many times, because the people involved share a genuine interest in what they do and are encouraged and rewarded for communicating.

Management has supported the community by making it easier for them to collaborate.

Tools: The real shop floor is devoted to precisely defined tasks, and is supported by highly specialised tools. Its lathes, metal punches, order book procedures, x-ray machines and fork lift trucks enable operatives to do their tasks in prescribed manners, at set speeds and to required standards.

The tools of knowledge creation, though, are general purpose items – telephones, computers, databases, paper and pencils, books and post-it notes. The virtual shop floor needs such flexible tools because its processes and outputs are so under-defined. People communicate about what interests and challenges them. The social nature of the virtual shop floor means that managers can never be sure which tools will be used.

More than that, the virtual shop floor may actively seek to avoid management. Two academic researchers, Niall Hayes and Geoff Walsham, examined intranet conferences for a UK-based pharmaceuticals firm that they called Compound UK. They discovered that the active involvement of senior managers in conferences caused salespersons to withdraw because they did not trust management enough to share their ideas with them. Knowledge sharing either ceased or found different tools because participants feared the possibility of being judged[10].

---

[10]Niall Hayes and Geoff Walsham, 'Safe havens and political enclaves'. Paper delivered to the First International Conference in Critical Management, Manchester Business School, 7–9 July 1999.

At IBM Global Services, knowledge management principal John Blackwell makes a special point of emphasising coffee room and water cooler gossip as core channels when presenting IBM's vision of knowledge management to potential clients.

IBM is not just selling the benefits of electronic communication systems. John Blackwell knows that people will continue to use other tools to share knowledge and that corporate knowledge management systems need to acknowledge and support them in order to be effective.

In their guide to knowledge management practices, Arthur Andersen describe how the Philadelphia-based engineering firm Day & Zimmerman split its head office between a city centre and suburban site six years ago, connecting the two with state-of-the-art electronics. Within three years suburban-based staff were relocated back to the city centre because the electronic communications system was not generating the quality and quantity of innovations that spontaneous face-to-face communications had produced before the split.

The real and virtual shop floors

	The real shop floor	The virtual shop floor
Place	Factory, office or shop	In people's heads, social environments
Participation	Formally defined roles and functions	Voluntary or ill-defined communities of practice. Level and quality of contributions are invisible
Communication	Face-to-face, routine, formal	Electronic or face-to-face, ad hoc
Tools	Machines, computers, stethoscopes, vehicles	Information systems, communications equipment, databases
Inputs	Defined mixtures of raw materials, capital and labour	Information that the knowledge worker defines as necessary

Processes	Physical, repetitive and linear systems	Intellectual, non-linear and social systems
Outputs	Common outputs in recognised form: reports, physical products, events	Unique information that may or may not be recognised: ideas, questions, solutions
Metrics	Visible, collected and objective	Hidden, dispersed and social

Processes: One of the most important elements in the management of the real shop floor is an understanding of the process of production. Michael Hammer and James Champy called attention to the processes of the real shop floor in *Re-engineering the Corporation* in 1993[11].

'We define a business process as a collection of activities that takes on one or more kinds of input and creates an output that is of value to the customer ... The individual tasks within this process are important, but none of them matters one whit if the overall process doesn't work – that is, if the process doesn't deliver the goods.'

Hammer and Champy's focus was on the efficiency of the overall process. Their solution, Business Process Re-engineering (BPR), requires precise knowledge of the system of tasks and inputs set against the criteria of customer requirements.

BPR is well and truly out of favour with many managers because the corporate downsizing and restructuring that it inspired appeared to leave many organisations worse off than when they started. This was because BPR initiatives involved the clear-out of many middle managers, people whose knowledge was badly missed when the re-engineered corporations came up against new situations that required systems to change. Real efficiency gains are all very well when organisational purpose is fixed and unchanging, but organisations depend on the virtual

---

[11] Michael Hammer and James Champy, *Reengineering the Corporation*, Nicholas Brealey, London, 1993.

shop floor to recognise and respond to environmental changes. Even the apparently unindustrial real shop floor where consultants work can be just as tightly controlled as an assembly line when, as often happens, management control is concentrated on the number of consultant days rather than the sought-after outcome of the consultancy exercise.

The problem is not with BPR. Rather, it is the failure of many corporate managers and BPR consultants to understand that there is a virtual shop floor as well as a real one. Its processes are intellectual, non-linear and social. Individuals and activities may appear unproductive on the real shop floor when, in fact, they are highly productive on the virtual shop floor. Many BPR projects turned into longer term disasters because of the short-sighted and naïve concentration of most projects on revising real shop floor processes without any awareness of the damage done to virtual shop floor processes.

The knowledge broker

The knowledge broker is a character found in every organisation. He/she is often a relatively unproductive real shop floor worker but is full of information about people, events in corporate history, obscure technical facts and client knowledge. The knowledge broker is a key player on the virtual shop floor because other people are able to learn and perform their functions better through interaction with them.

There was such a character in the planning office of a district in Yorkshire during the 1980's. Kelvyn could never stop poking into issues that did not directly concern him and had a desk piled high with work he had not completed on time. He was continually criticised by management for poor performance and ultimately was forced out of his job.

Until he left, though, there was not a single key research project team or task group that did not consult him. The same managers who were trying to get rid of him would instruct researchers to *'start with Kelvyn.'* It was always worth doing. Kelvyn's weakness was that the nature of his effectiveness showed up on the virtual shop floor where too few knew to look. Using existing measures, too much of his contribution was reflected in the performance of others.

The processes of the virtual shop floor are problematic because most aspects of the virtual system are invisible. Its successes show up discontinuously as real shop floor achievements that may be widely removed in time and space from the initial knowledge creating activity. At Canon, the revolutionary idea in ink cartridge design was inspired by a beer break. Jerry Hirshberg's response to a corporate creative block at Nissan Design International was to take the whole company to see *Silence of the Lambs,* spontaneously closing the whole building during a working day.

Inputs, outputs and metrics: Stakeholders require the achievement of visible goals of productivity, profitability, sales and so on. Indeed, the ultimate purpose of information and knowledge in organisations is success on the real shop floor. As a result, individuals and departments are judged against quantified targets. Teams in organisations are usually set up with 'hard' purposes that are measurable and measured.

The whole basis of the management of the real shop floor is that inputs and outputs can be precisely quantified and valued. Annual accounts contain the chairman's and managing director's reports on the many qualitative achievements of the past year, but what really matters is the quantified profit and loss account. Unsurprisingly, the most certain route to the top of corporations today is through accountancy, that is, the management discipline that focuses on the measuring and managing of the inputs and outputs of the real shop floor.

The virtual shop floor is a wholly different animal, though, because its inputs, outputs and metrics are so much more difficult to quantify. The knowledge generated by an individual or team may contribute to achievements in ways that go unrecognised or have nothing to do with the immediate purpose or focus of the people involved. Knowledge brokers such as Kelvyn, for example, may be undervalued or even discarded because employers are unable to measure the worth of their contributions, even when their usefulness is informally recognised throughout the organisation.

Take Nissan Design International's visit to the movies, the precise cost in salary time, theatre tickets and popcorn can be worked out, but how are the benefits to be identified? Hirshberg quotes an enquiry from an *AutoWeek* journalist, *'We'd like to know the connection between serial murder and car design.'* So should everyone who visualises organisations only as real shop floors. Hirshberg wanted to ease the pressure on his designers by taking them away from their 'real' need to meet a design deadline. He knew that the real shop floor was where the output would emerge, but he was more concerned to manage the hidden knowledge processes needed to enable it.

The chief knowledge officers

In 1998 Michael Earl and Ian Scott of the London Business School undertook a survey of chief knowledge officers. After an extensive search, they estimated that there were only 25 in North America and Europe[12]. They used two conditions to define them:

1. They had to have 'knowledge' in their title, to demonstrate an explicit organisational commitment to thinking about and managing knowledge as opposed to information or other corporate resources.
2. They had to be senior executives and leading explicit corporate-wide knowledge programmes.

---

[12] Michael Earl and Ian Scott, 'What on earth is a CKO?', London Business School, 1998.

Earl and Scott found that chief knowledge officers mainly managed small teams with small budgets. Their roles were fourfold:

- to develop a corporate knowledge management vision
- to promote the knowledge management agenda by familiarising and persuading managers to adopt knowledge models, frameworks and language
- to oversee development of knowledge infrastructures
- to support and encourage appropriate knowledge-oriented communication within and without the organisation.

The reasons for these functions reflect the blend of different perspectives that organisations bring to defining their purpose in seeking to manage knowledge. Earl and Scott warned that managers in a sizeable minority of organisations see knowledge as information, so that knowledge management is viewed merely as an extension of information management.

Conclusion – the management challenge of the virtual shop floor

The objective of introducing the virtual shop floor is to make clear that knowledge management is not a new and separate managerial concern. The virtual shop floor has always existed alongside and intertwined with the real shop floor. It is the focus and managerial challenge of knowledge management.

Managers are, understandably, happiest with processes that produce predictable outputs. The problem with knowledge creation processes is that there is no guarantee that they will produce the desired results. New knowledge is like a wrapped gift. It may be the golf clubs you asked for or the unexpected trip of a lifetime to Tahiti. Equally, it could be yet another awful tie with a horse's head pattern. There are no guarantees.

Some experienced managers may feel that the management challenge is to make the virtual shop floor more visible, so it can be controlled like the real one, while others may want to encourage the development of the virtual shop floor. One of the main purposes of this book is to warn that either approach has both merit and weakness, depending on the situation. According to Doctor Allan Taylor of Abertay University in Scotland, '*A decision has to be made about when it is better to capture and make real [virtual shop floor functions].*'

There are some situations where it is beyond dispute that virtual shop floor activity can and should be made real so it can be more tightly controlled. These are mainly where a single best approach has been recognised that is unlikely to be improved on. The tragic collision of an inter-city express train and a local commuter train near Paddington Station in October 1999 occurred after one of the trains passed a red signal light. It is generally accepted that it is always right that trains do not pass red signals, so there is no obvious knowledge benefit in leaving the decision to the judgement of train drivers.

In most cases, though, the situation is less clear cut. Sometimes, for instance in many telesales operations, operatives are required to follow explicit scripts and are tightly monitored. Such control assumes that one approach is best for all sales people and all potential customers. It limits the possibility of new and more individual styles emerging and may dissatisfy the untypical customer, but it enables staff to handle a high volume of calls rapidly and may prevent illegal high-pressure sales practices.

Knowledge management tools and programmes are already plentiful on the market. They are mainly software packages that support logical and linear knowledge practices. Almost all of them will disappoint – mechanical miracle cures for a uniquely human and desirable condition, our capacity to create and share spontaneously and positively. Elizabeth Lank changed her title from Chief Knowledge Officer at ICL to *Programme Director, Mobilising Knowledge*, in order to drive home to her colleagues that she was not the manager of a thing called knowledge, but the facilitator of

ICL's knowledge process development. Cap Gemini sends the same message by calling its knowledge management consultancy *Knowledge Transformation Services.*

Ultimately, the knowledge management challenge is about finding better ways to tap into and support the creative potential of the people in organisations. John Seely Brown of Xerox PARC offers this advice to '*hard-nosed CEOs*' who cannot see the point of woolly virtual shop floor management[13].

'This is exactly the kind of story that can make sense to CEO's... Knowledge creation for the firm and knowledge sharing for the firm lead to the construction of meaning for the individual and construction of social capital for the community of practice. Together they give you the winning formula...Trying to divorce the one from the other actually increases the difficulty of your job. ... One of the reasons that corporations seldom have long lives is because the knowledge dynamics of the firm have never been understood.'

---

[13] John Seely Brown, 'Conversation' (with Don Cohen), *Knowledge Directions,* Vol. 1, Spring 1999.

2

Better information management is not enough

Introduction

There is not a chief executive alive who has not at some time said, *'Our people are our most important assets.'* While applauding the sentiment, I wonder, *'Why? What makes them so valuable?'* It cannot be their capacity to fulfil their job descriptions, because all the evidence suggests that almost no job matches its description in practice. What makes them so important is the way that they exceed or ignore their job descriptions to better achieve their jobs' purposes. They think, learn, create and share in ways that no list of duties can hope to capture or confine. That is what makes them so valuable.

Having sat together and heard the same evidence, juries are often evenly divided between those who find defendants guilty and those who find them innocent. In order to go further in knowledge management, we need to understand what causes this to happen. Clearly, there are times when shared information does not lead to shared knowledge. Otherwise there would never be any hung juries.

Why is it that the same information means different things to different people? In this chapter we explore and explain the implications of the fact that information has no purpose or worth until people find meaning in it. We go to the heart of the question, *What exactly is knowledge?* It is essential to do this early in the knowledge management journey to avoid drifting into the trap of treating knowledge as a kind of 'better' information, that simply needs better information management.

Knowledge work and knowledge workers

Throughout the book, the terms 'knowledge work' and 'knowledge worker' are used. Knowledge work is, simply, the process of learning, sharing and creating that accompanies the doing of tasks by individuals and teams. The less routine the task, the more intensive and important the knowledge work is likely to be. Anyone can be, and is, a knowledge worker at some time, but usually the extent to which one can be considered a knowledge worker rises with the variety of the tasks performed. The less repetition there is in a job, the more decision-making and the more teamwork, are all indicators of knowledge work.

There is nothing especially new about such observations. Why has knowledge management suddenly appeared and become important now not fifty years ago? The simple answer is that information and communication technologies offer the prospect of leveraging the capacity of people to be *important resources* as never before. The critical role of knowledge, and the need for corporations to act knowledgeably, has become more apparent. Organisations need to manage the factors which are central to their future.

The first step in managing knowledge is to understand the elements of knowledge work. This requires that we explore what is meant by the terms 'information' and 'knowledge', and consider how information and knowledge are related to each other through knowledge work. Information is the input and reshaped information is the output of an organisation's knowledge processes, just as physical materials and parts are the inputs and manufactured goods are the outputs of a production line. Information *and* knowledge – information management is not enough.

Wait till we get information management right!

Managers are so familiar with information management that the definition of information is usually taken for granted, but a moment's thought soon leads to uncertainty. If, for instance, information is a set of known facts or truths, why is disagreement about 'the facts' so common? The world is full of completely contradictory 'truths'. It gets worse with knowledge. How do we know what we know? And how do we separate trivial knowledge from what is important; particularly when what you think is important seems trivial to others?

The first group to which I formally introduced knowledge management was a forum of middle and senior managers with IT and internal communications responsibilities in some of the biggest, electronically enabled 'virtual corporations' in the world. They were not impressed. As one put it, *'We're having enough trouble managing information and probably won't move on to knowledge management until we get information management right.'*

But, how will they know when that is? Ask yourself what constitutes a *'right'* information system? You will probably describe a system full of up-to-date, relevant and easily accessible information. You will know that you have a *'right'* system, not by stock-taking the information on it or by listing system technical capacities, but by auditing how it is used. If your people regularly employ the information system to help them develop and share what they know in order to achieve the organisation's core objectives as quickly and easily as possible, you can be confident that the system works. In other words, you will know that the information system is working when you can see evidence that it is supporting knowledge work. Your judgement will be based on the effective performance of the organisation and not on the technical performance of the information system. In the case overleaf of the Mars Climate Orbiter, a corporate disaster resulted from the efficient operation of an information system, because the scientists who used it drew different lessons from shared information.

Houston, we have a problem...

The Mars Climate Orbiter was a triumphant example of teamwork between different organisations and an important element in America's on-going exploration of Mars. The key to its success was the way that the teams at Lockheed Martin Astronautics in Denver, Colorado, and the Jet Propulsion Laboratory in Pasadena, California, shared information. At least that is how it seemed two years into its epic voyage in September 1999, until the moment it came time for the rockets to delicately nudge the multi-million dollar orbiter into place above Mars...

However, as Doctor Susanne Tietze of Nottingham Business School points out, *'The meanings that we intend in the messages we send may not be the same as the meanings attached by the people who receive our messages. They attach their own meanings.'* It turns out that the team in Denver was working in English units (pounds and inches) while the Californians were using metric units (newtons and millimetres). The teams never questioned each other's understanding of the information they shared.

Alas, for the Mars Climate Orbiter, *'Our inability to recognise and correct this simple error has had major implications'*, as said Dr. Edward Stone, director of the Jet Propulsion Laboratory. Instead of a delicate nudge, the Climate Orbiter computers asked for an enormous blast of rocket power which sent it far into the depths of space.

A good information management system helps ensure that the capacity to do knowledge work is enhanced, but it does not actually cause the work to get done. Businesses will never *'get information management right'* until they understand its connection with knowledge work. The information system is there to supply the materials (information) that employees need to develop and apply their knowledge, and to receive, store and distribute the new information that they generate. As such, it acts as a kind of materials handling system supporting knowledge work.

In a very real sense, knowledge workers should be seen as the people who create and reshape information into new forms just as craftsmen create and reshape physical materials into more valuable products. The primary difference is that the virtual shop floor is inside people's heads, on their computer screens and within their teams. The knowledge environment is not a physical place. The information system supplies the logistics support to the virtual shop floor – warehousing, classification and delivery – that makes knowledge work more fruitful, just as efficient physical logistics are essential to manufacturing.

Between 1997 and 1999 IBM actually cut its investment in information technology by a third, by switching its attention from the management of information to the use of information in support of the application of knowledge. Much of their previous investment in information management became redundant, while their on-going investment became more effectively focused on its true purpose, to enable knowledge work.

The image of the virtual shop floor is useful, because more and more companies in all sorts of markets and industries are styling themselves as 'knowledge-intensive' or 'knowledge-based' organisations, much as they once called themselves manufacturing or service companies. They still manufacture and they still deliver services, but they call attention to what sets them apart from the competition – their knowledge.

The information trap

Anyone can get information. There is an ocean of it slopping around the Internet, our libraries and our files. The trick is to learn from it, share it, create from it and, generally, do all the communal things that make us and organisations succeed. That is knowledge work and it is the focus of knowledge management.

Those managers who remain focused on ever more sophisti-
cated information storage and communication systems are
missing the point. Most of their employees have all the information they want and a lot more that they don't want.
Information is the wrong target. Information is only useful if it
engages our brains. Logically, the more information we get, the
more of our attention and time is used up. Managers need to
allocate time and attention between the growing volume of
competing pieces of information. Which reports do they read?
What statistics do they study?

Picture the Hewlett-Packard sales executive in the north of
England who was receiving more than 120 messages *per day* early
in 1998, or the senior BT executive receiving an average of 150
messages per day in the spring of 1999. Information is stopping
them from doing their jobs. The BT executive has had to develop
guidelines for her team to identify and eliminate probably irrelevant messages. *'We used to warn or even sack people for not reading
their messages. In a year we've turned a dismissable offence into an
approved coping strategy.'* Another senior analyst had just left a
major IT company, claiming that his job involved *'three and a half
days of responding to e-mails, and another day and a half to do **proper
work**.'*

Sue Honore, of the Oxfordshire-based training and learning
consultancy Espace, describes a personal coping strategy for
handling more than 200 daily messages, when she worked for a
global microchip supplier. It will be familiar to most executives.
*'You become a very good filterer of e-mails and read only titles. My approach
was to delete every message that did not look interesting or important before
I had opened it. If I deleted a really important message without reading it,
I assumed that the sender would phone or come to my desk. Even so, I used
to get into work an hour early and leave an hour late.'*

Controlling the flow of information

One of the main challenges in information management is to
develop efficient tools to limit the flow of information, and so help

workers preserve their time for generating profits. There probably is not an intranet-connected employee in the world who does not know the feeling of oppression that comes with the long line of little red flags that is almost the first thing they see on their screen each morning. Yet, as Davenport and Prusak point out[1], it is the recipient of a message who turns it into information by being informed by it. If he is too busy to read it or understand it, then it is just meaningless data.

Data is perceived as information as long as it possesses certain qualities. Information is data that (1) fits with your understanding of reality, (2) is useful, and (3) can be communicated[2]. Looking at each of these points in turn:

1. It is grounded in your understanding of reality

The first thing about information is that it must be believable. We know what will happen to us if we are caught in a rainstorm without an umbrella because we are familiar with our environment. Rain has taught us to expect to get wet. A friend, Patrick Nurse, arrived in England as an eight year-old from Barbados. He tells a vivid story of the morning when he awoke to find a white carpet spread over everything outside. Not waiting to dress, he ran into the back garden and was shocked to discover that the carpet was cold and wet. He had read about snow and seen pictures of it, but it took the shock to his feet for him to know snow. Until that moment, the information about snow was unbelievable because it was ungrounded.

When British Leyland Automobiles opened an engine plant in South Wales in the 1960's, many of its new employees were ex-miners who were accustomed to working far underground[3]. They

---

[1] Thomas H. Davenport and Laurence Prusak, *Working Knowledge*, Harvard Business School Press, 1998.

[2] For a detailed discussion of the psychological basis of the argument that follows, you should read:
Frank Blackler, 'Knowledge, knowledge work and organisation: an overview and interpretation', *Organisation Studies*, 16/6, 1995.

[3] E. Belbin and R.M. Belbin, *Problems in Adult Training*, Heinemann, 1972.

were conscientious and high quality workers, but too slow and careful for the assembly line. They had to unlearn their previously justified belief that safety required that they kept one eye on the floors, walls and roof in case they suddenly shifted, a highly grounded attitude in a deep coal mine.

People reject data that does not fit with their world view because it does not make sense to them. Psychologists call the emotions and thoughts caused by such data *cognitive dissonance*. In effect, if information clashes with what we already know and trust, we do not believe it and cannot believe it without changing our view of the world.

The unsinkable ship

There are some notorious historic examples of cognitive dissonance in history. I am distantly related to Edward Smith, who captained the SS *Titanic*. Captain Smith sailed it at full-speed into an iceberg, because everyone knew the *Titanic* was an unsinkable ship with no need to worry about icebergs. The nearby SS *California* did not bother to respond to the *Titanic's* distress flares for the same reason, dismissing them as a fireworks display. It was inconceivable that the mighty *Titanic* could be in trouble where the ordinary *California* was not.

In business, the most visible evidence of cognitive dissonance comes from what Harvard Business School's Clayton Christiansen calls *disruptive innovation*. Most organisations are capable of improving what they already do to better serve the markets that they already serve. These '*sustaining innovations*' do not force them to change the way they look at the world.

Profoundly new ideas, though, are rarely taken up by established corporations, because they challenge dominant corporate notions of reality. Not one of the world's major steel producers responded to the rise of minimills by building one themselves, despite clear evidence that minimills were nearly four times as efficient[4]. Nucor and Chaparral grew fat on the inability of the strategists at Republic, US and British Steel to conceive that small facilities could make steel competitively. At Digital Equipment Corporation (DEC) the dominant mini-computer manufacturer of twenty years ago, management dismissed the personal computer as no threat to its market dominance and failed to set up a separate personal computer division until 1993, when the market was long gone. DEC is no more, swallowed up by Compaq.

It takes a fundamental leap of imagination to disrupt your understanding of reality, and only a few major corporations have done it. IBM, having been the overwhelmingly dominant mainframe computer supplier, nearly sank under the weight of attack from mini-computer and hardware systems competition. In 1993 it generated the largest ever reported corporate loss, over $14 billion. Its solution was to completely reinvent itself as a supplier of business solutions, a consultancy, rather than a computer manufacturer. It stopped using its business solutions knowledge to support its business focus on hardware sales and began using its hardware capabilities to support its new focus on supplying business solutions. Hewlett-Packard made a similar fundamental shift in the printer sector, when it moved from laser printing to inkjet technology.

2. It is useful

A second key element that defines information is its usefulness. There is far too much data around to save it all. Something is only useful information to those who can see a purpose for it. If data does not serve a purpose for the person who possesses it, then it has no value. A designer from Spokane is unlikely to be informed by data about the pop music industry in Pakistan unless he is designing a product that requires such information. We refer to useless information as 'trivia.' The only people who remember it are pub quiz champions or players of Trivial Pursuit. For them, it is useful.

---

[4] See Clayton Christiansen, *The Innovator's Dilemma*, Harvard Business School, 1997, for this interesting case study.

A pointed criticism of most business studies degrees is that subject matter often seems obscure or even irrelevant to the students. In part this is because some lecturers may not have enough practical experience of what they are teaching to communicate it meaningfully to their students, or that young students simply lack enough experience of business to appreciate a subject's relevance, however well it is taught. As a result, what is studied can seem unreal and be forgotten as soon as the exams end. The students who come to their studies with at least a year of work experience are both the best learners and the most perceptively critical ones, because they have had a year in which to discover how learning can be useful in a work context.

We do not always recognise useful information for what it is. Jonathan Cooper, a young entrepreneur in Yorkshire, opened his first high fashion clothes store in Sheffield after eight months of business planning in 1993. From the start, it was a disaster. The wrong location, the wrong product line and poor in-store presentation combined to bring the business to its knees. Jonathan had to abandon his plan and strike out in a completely new direction. Jonathan says that what saved his business was not the plan, a document full of irrelevant and inaccurate information, but the knowledge he acquired about running a business during the planning process and the time spent trying to follow the plan. That gave him the insight to understand when real experience turned out wildly different from the unrealistic scenario in his business plan. He had learned how to think critically about his business during the planning stage, but needed the real life experience of operating stores to make his ideas truly pragmatic. Today, Alley Fashions is profitable and growing.

Often, potentially useful information is made available at the wrong time. When I worked in an economic development consultancy a few years ago there was a staged move into a new desktop computer system. To save money and time, we were all trained half way through the four month investment process. Those who had their computers first had already learned much of the course content through trial-and-error. Those who had a month or more to wait for their new computers forgot most of the content. Only people who had just received or were about to receive their new machines felt that the training had pragmatic value.

Information may be useless because it offers a use which seems irrelevant to its recipient. When staff receive a general e-mail about parking rights in the office car park it provides useful information to those who drive to work but is a time-wasting red flag to those who catch the train or bus.

A famous organisational illustration of the way that recipients decide the usefulness of information comes from Xerox Corporation. Xerox's famous research facility at Palo Alto (Xerox PARC) provided very little return for Xerox when it made the breakthroughs in screen technology that enabled the development of the personal computer, but was a goldmine of information for Steve Jobs, the micro-computer pioneer, who applied what he learned from visiting PARC to set up Apple. The key to usefulness is in the perspective of the person or organisation that possesses the information. Xerox was a reprographics firm and could not see itself in the computer industry. Steve Jobs was an entrepreneur who could imagine a world of personal computers.

3. It can be communicated

Finally, information must be communicable. What this means is that information must be describable in a way that more than one person can understand. I had a teacher once who showed the class a volume of Shakespeare's plays in Chinese and asked if it was great literature. When everyone said that it was, he asked us to prove it. Not reading Chinese, we could not. The Bard in Chinese had nothing to teach us.

As in literature, so in business. A decade ago, a collaborative project between academics from Sheffield Business School and the University of Franche-Comte came to nothing because lecturers failed to appreciate that the ability to speak a foreign language does not solve all the difficulties of foreign language communication. They did not realise that the often undiplomatic exchanges were due to inadequate familiarity with foreign vocabularies and could not make criticisms sound constructive in each other's languages. Differences sounded more profound than they really were.

It is not just that we speak different national tongues, we also speak different professional languages and attach different technical meanings to the same words. As recently as 1998 at one global telecommunications giant, for instance, a team looking at employee retention found seventeen different definitions for termination date within the company. These ranged from first notification of termination through to the actual moment when physical employment ceased and on to the date when severance pay was deemed to no longer apply for tax purposes. At another, they had five different definitions of starting date[5].

Even when the decision has been taken to use just one language, it does not follow that communication will be better mediated. At yet another corporate information system provider, employees became accustomed to using other communications media to bypass the inadequate intranet. Corporate efforts to increase its usage became more and more intensive. Between 1996 and 1999 it was being renewed more or less continuously. In the end, that was the problem. A survey of key staff across Europe revealed that a whole range of ad hoc and unmanaged systems had grown up to enable people to do their jobs. They knew that their private systems were inefficient, but at least their stability could be trusted.

> 'Crucially, knowledge management is not about accessing even more information. Rather, it's about having more relevant information and contacts, to create better ideas. It's about exchanging knowledge in a more effective way.'
>
> Tom Boyle
> Chief Learning Manager, BT UK, Human Resources

---

[5] Both cases were described to me by members of the Electronic Communication Forum. Their anonymity is maintained to spare their blushes, but this kind of definitional confusion is very common.

A core challenge in knowledge management is ensuring that the information that could be of value to the organisation is widely shared. This requires more than an efficient and effective information system. It requires that employees understand the importance of their information and have the will and means to share it as well. The opportunity cost of not communicating can be enormous. Often, the main causes of lost contracts and dissatisfied customers are telephone messages not passed on or unforwarded e-mails within organisations. Equally, messages that are passed on may not be received or may be misunderstood.

When the Challenger space shuttle blew up in 1986 it was due to the failure of a rubber seal. The risk of such a failure was widely reported within the NASA information system *and was even discussed on the day of the launch*. Whatever else went wrong in the lead up to the Challenger tragedy, the information system performed perfectly.

> *First principle:* The value of information is determined by its recipients and not by its senders. If we don't receive it, understand it, don't believe it or cannot see a use for it, it is worthless data.

Information – food for thought

Imagine information as food. When you are starving you collect whatever you can find. You eat and benefit from every edible scrap. Otherwise, you grow weak and undernourished. You become less good at doing things in competition with other food collectors and, ultimately, you sicken and die.

Suppose that the harvests get better. Your problem changes from one of collection to one of selection. You need to eat what is good for you and ignore the rest. Just like the starving person, the overfed one slows down, sickens and dies. The people who thrive are the ones who eat healthily, while leaving the cream cakes and high cholesterol to others. The best survival strategy is to concentrate on the most nourishing food, something that you cannot do without a deep understanding of how your body uses different kinds of food.

Corporate information systems are supplying ever-growing mountains of food for thought to executives and it is more than they can handle. They need an efficient means of identifying, sharing and consuming it. To complicate matters, what nourishes one person is very likely to sicken another. Information systems can generate more food for thought than we can use.

Assessing information systems

Information systems have been studied for a long time, but for the most part information management has had a system orientation. This approach views information as having a content that is fixed and the same for whoever views it. The focus of interest is on the system rather than the information it contains. More recently, attention has switched towards the users of information. A user orientation assumes that, whatever the objective content of a piece of information, its meaning to the user will decide how important it is.

System orientation makes the task of information management simpler, because information managers need only concentrate on rational systems for the efficient collection and movement of information. It would be perfectly adequate if only people used information like they use other resources, for defined purposes in designated places.

User orientation makes the task harder, because the system has to be able to respond to the views of the users. A rational system will not necessarily work because people in organisations are not rational. In the words of Karl Weick[6], they *'oppose, argue, contradict, disbelieve, doubt, act hypocritically, improvise, counter, distrust, differ, challenge, vacillate, question, puncture, disprove and expose.'*

A simple test of the compatability with knowledge management of a corporate information system is to assess whether it is orientated towards users or towards itself. Ask yourself:

1. Does the information system fail to recognise the many different, and often, informal ways that people prefer to send and receive information?
2. Is the quantity of information on the system growing faster than the capacity to use it?
3. Does the average person put more information into the system (serving it) than they get out of the system (being served by it).

Just one 'yes' answer points away from a user orientation and towards a system orientation. It promises serious problems for your people. Knowledge management requires a user orientation in information management.

The efficient virtual shop floor

The Internet, satellite television, fast air travel, international co-operation about trade regulations and standards, all of these now mean that almost any organisation has the potential to develop useful knowledge about practically every market in the world.

---

[6] Karl Weick, *The Social Psychology of Organizing*, Addison-Wesley, 1979.

The comparative popularity of soft drinks in Malaysia, the social implications of support for Glasgow Celtic and Glasgow Rangers soccer clubs, or the clothes buying habits in post-apartheid South Africa, are all knowable around the world.

The advantage is no longer in having more information, but in using the same information more effectively than everyone else. When almost every virtual shop floor has access to the same information, it is the efficiency and effectiveness with which it processes and uses the information that matters. The challenge of knowledge management is to refine our focus so that we only generate and share the most nutritious information. Previously, when information was much less plentiful, the primary concern was how much information could be collected; now the main challenge is processing and using information, as illustrated in the figure below.

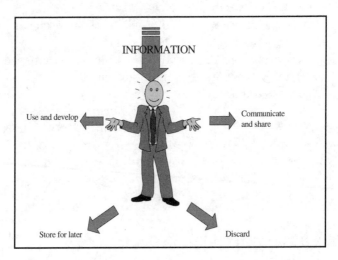

In 1998 I was asked to advise a corporation about a proposal to build a new intranet. It quickly became apparent that, whatever the advice, a new system was going to be put in place as quickly as possible, without serious examination of the nature and working of the corporate virtual shop floor. It seemed astonishing that the corporate sponsors of the project accepted without comment the project team's observation that, '… *many companies have found themselves in a similar position to SG* (a pseudonym) *and are currently building their intranets a second, third or even fourth time around.'*

Such a resigned acceptance of mediocrity is an open invitation to competitors. As long as every virtual shop floor goes unmanaged, a corporation's performance may not stand out as particularly poor, but a gap is emerging between what most companies are doing and what effective knowledge management could achieve. The longer organisations fail to manage knowledge, the more attractive the opportunity for someone else to do it will become.

One of the most frequently quoted stories in every basic international marketing course is the tale of General Motors' launch of the Nova onto the Mexican market in the 1970's. The only advantage that General Motors' competitors needed to see off the Nova was basic high school Spanish (Nova = No go).

In how many major world markets today is mere knowledge of the language enough to confer a killing competitive advantage? John D. Brennan, Associate Partner at Andersen Consulting, calls the notion that information confers profound advantages *'an industrial-age economic assumption.'* He warns that the opportunities for profit arising from imperfect information are growing fewer.

What do we mean by knowledge?

At this point, you may well be scratching your head. So, information is not knowledge; what exactly is knowledge? It would be no problem, if along with Sergeant Joe Friday of the old *Dragnet* TV series, we could ask for *'just the facts, ma'am.'* But, as the example overleaf demonstrates, even the experts cannot always be trusted.

Ask the experts

Josephine Klein wrote in 1961 about a research project which involved asking members of the British Psychological Society to report what they could remember of a meeting they had just attended. *'Upon analysis, it was found that only about a tenth of the points that had been made were recalled in the reports. Of these, nearly half were "substantially incorrect". Both logical and emotional factors had led the members of the Society to recall events which had never happened, and further distortions were due to omissions, exaggerations or plain muddle-headedness. On average, a member recalled about three times as many of his own points as points made by other people. The average member was, however, no more accurate about himself than he was about others.'*

Josephine Klein, 'Working with groups',
Hutchinson University Library, 1961

Most of us think of knowledge as 'facts that are known', or 'things that are true'. The trouble is that the knowledge of different people is so contradictory. Knowledge is simply too personal a thing to be reduced to a set of 'true facts'. How else can we explain the endless meetings in which people disagree and argue passionately, because they *know* they are right? Here is a set of quotes from sessions I have facilitated or observed recently:

'What he's saying is just an opinion! It's not mine.'

'The facts are there, but you have to have the right experience to understand them.'

'The results are a fluke. The data must be wrong.'

'I don't believe that we can trust the information without first hand experience to back it up.'

'We didn't find that the briefing notes were any help at all. This is what it is really like.'

'*Has anyone stopped to ask why we believe the market won't accept a two day turn around?*'

'*Call it a gut instinct or past experience, I don't think it will work.*'

Knowledge is justified belief

All of the quotes are about knowledge and lead us towards a two word definition. Knowledge is *justified belief*[7]. Each of the two words is important and so are the words like *truthful* and *objective* that are left out. Knowledge is rarely objective and truth is rarely uncontested. Looking at each part of the definition in turn:

Knowledge is justified

This is when our experience or the experience of people we trust supports what we know. When Tony Hales took on the CE role at Allied-Lyons in 1991, he set out to expand its world-wide brand presence through alliances with other regionally strong brands. Allied Domecq, its spirits manufacturing subsidiary, built up its market share from less than 1% to more than 20% in only four years. In Hale's words[8], 'Normally our expertise would be in brands and technology, and our partner's would be local distribution and market knowledge. It requires a mutual respect...'

IBM Global Services has not just focused its marketing on knowledge management, it has restructured itself as a knowledge manager. IBM knowledge management consultants don't just sell a product; they sell the way IBM is. As John Blackwell, principal for knowledge management, puts it, 'Our clients know we believe in it, because we are doing it ourselves.'

Unjustified belief, on the other hand, is not knowledge, but blind faith. Corporate histories are littered with stories of products and investments that were built on unjustified belief. Amongst the more famous is the Ford Edsel, which was just bound to sell

---

[7] Ikujira Nonaka and H. Takeuchi, *The Knowledge Creating Company*, Oxford University Press, 1996.

[8] Quoted in an interview to William Kay, *The Bosses*, Piatkus, 1994.

after Ford pumped millions into every aspect of its launch in the late 1950's. Everything that was done, all the development and market research, was based on the certain belief that it would succeed. After so much expenditure it had to sell! If only someone had told the market, the Edsel was the least successful car launch in automotive history.

Wishful thinking frequently hides reality from our sight and creates a spurious justification. At a meeting of British coal industry economists in 1986, it was agreed that there was little chance that the government would privatise the electricity sector until after it had disposed of the nationalised coal industry. I attended that meeting and, afterwards, wrote a report saying just that, circulated to all ninety members of the coal field communities association that I directed. Alas, electricity privatisation was announced within months, catching me and the association (those reassured by my blinkered report!) entirely by surprise. The coal industry limped along in the public sector for five more years. If only some economists from outside the coal industry had been at that meeting, I might have heard at least one opinion from someone whose job did not depend on coal being privatised before electricity.

Knowledge is belief

Belief is the second key. However much evidence there is, something only becomes knowledge through belief. This is important, because everyone sees the world differently. What you think of as truth is unlikely to agree in every particular with what I think. One of the most consistent causes of project failure is the solution or system developed by a consultant or another department and 'parachuted in.' The people are told that the solution will work, are trained in it and then reject it.

'It would work perfectly, but no one's willing to give it a chance!'[9] said the young webmaster of a market information company last year, when reviewing a poorly used intranet. He

---

[9] This is known as **The Webmaster's Lament**.

believed in the system because he had been intimately involved in its development, but most of his colleagues did not.

In the mid 1980's, Bill Gates invited IBM to buy into Microsoft. He needed funding to continue the development of the Windows operating system and wanted to avoid the approaching commercial war that was threatened by IBM's launch of its own operating system, OS2. IBM managers knew the market as well as Microsoft and learned how Gates thought the market would develop. Unfortunately, they did not believe what he told them. His knowledge was not transferred to IBM, because *you cannot know something that you do not believe.*

Returning to the 1986 Challenger space shuttle explosion, caused by failure of a part called the O-ring which had been supplied by Thiokol, it emerged that[10]:

'*Roger Boisjoly, a staff engineer knowledgeable about the O-rings, had warned that the quality of the damage on the January 1985 launch was worse because "the putty looked different in other instances of blow-by." NASA management saw this as an intuitive argument that was not substantially supported. Thiokol engineers acknowledged that their argument was subjective and based on engineering feel. Because of the inability to convert and share this tacit knowledge the warning signals remained weak and confused and could not raise doubt about the assumption of O-ring redundancy [margin of safety]... At 11.38 the following morning the Challenger was launched... Seconds later, the shuttle exploded killing all on board.'*

After the fact, it was clear that Boisjoly's information should have been believed. However, before the fact, with millions of dollars worth of investment and the television cameras of the world watching (Challenger was part of a series of space flights which were aimed at raising NASA's public relations profile), there were too many reasons not to believe.

---

[10]For a more complete discussion see C.W. Choo, *The Knowing Organization*, pp. 155–164, Sage, London, 1998.

Knowledge is not objective truth

But what of the words not included in the definition? As the examples demonstrate, justified belief does not imply objective truth. One thing history teaches is that the truth is always changing. There is no such thing, for instance, as the best product on the market. There is only the one that customers prefer at the moment. In 1906, the Stanley steam-powered automobile achieved 127 mph, more than twice as fast as cars powered by internal combustion, but the market rejected it. There can be few things more certain than that Apple and Windows operating system users each know that their system is easier and more user-friendly than the other. Their beliefs are justified by their personal experiences.

The blind shrimp of the deeps

When French oceanographer Jacques Cousteau began exploring the depths of the mid-ocean trenches, scientists were enthralled by the life forms discovered living on the edges of undersea volcanoes in the pitch black. Entirely blind, they somehow survived in ways that we could only guess. Forty years of underseas research gave no clues as to how the sightless shrimp got about.

Then, a breakthrough. Someone finally realised that the ocean floor was so dark that the lights that scientists needed to observe the shrimp were completely burning out their delicate sight systems. In other words, the shrimp could see, until scientists started checking if they could see! The only blind shrimp were the ones being studied. They were only blind because scientists studied them. The unstudied shrimp can still see, presumably.

In this case, scientific belief, that was justified by forty years of research, turned out not to be objective truth. Yet, the scientific community 'knew' that the shrimp were blind.

The problems that people have in understanding the difference between information and knowledge make it particularly difficult for them to conceptualise knowledge management. They are more comfortable with 'hard facts.' It is much easier to wrestle with production and sales figures from the real shop floor than to deal with uncertain meanings and social outputs from the virtual shop floor.

Conclusion – the management challenge of information

In this chapter we have developed definitions of information and knowledge.

Information is data that is grounded in your view of reality, that is useful in some way and can be communicated to others. If none of these applies, then it becomes meaningless data.

Knowledge is justified belief. Our knowledge is what we believe to be true, because our experience appears to justify it. It does not matter that others reject our justified beliefs, because our knowledge is purely subjective.

The chapter introduced the first guiding principle of knowledge management. Information is only useful if it is used. It is knowledge processes that turn information into valuable resources. We cannot be satisfied with efficient information management if our knowledge processes are inadequate. The real test of an information system is how well it serves the actual workings of knowledge workers on the virtual shop floor.

First principle: The value of information is determined by its recipients and not by its senders. If they don't understand it, don't believe it or cannot see a use for it, it is worthless data.

In our information-rich age, the mere possession of information by an organisation is not the same as using it productively. Knowledge is 'justified belief'. People do not know something just because they are informed of it. We only know things because they somehow enrich our lives. In an organisational context that means that the information enables us to perform tasks, mix with colleagues, achieve personal and organisational goals or otherwise derive meaning from the information. More than that, the same information can be interpreted in different but equally valuable ways by different people and different organisations.

The principles point towards an essential element in managing information and in understanding its connection with knowledge management. Information only has value in its use, so information management must be based on the perspective of those who demand information and not of those who supply it. Information management's task is to serve knowledge processes. Our knowledge enables us to interpret and to find value in information that others have created in ways that reflect our different circumstances and perceptions.

Too many information systems are designed without regard for the difference between the possession and the use of information. It is the use of information that gives it value. One of the challenges in knowledge management is to ensure that corporate information systems reflect and support its effective use. The mere possession of information brings no real benefit.

3

The knowledge creation cycle

Introduction

In this chapter we begin to explore in depth the workings of the virtual shop floor, concentrating on the relationship between information and knowledge. The explosion in the availability of information has placed ever-increasing pressures on knowledge workers, a knowledge bottleneck, in part because knowledge work is so poorly understood and appreciated.

The chapter explores how knowledge work has been overlooked because of the way that it can be hidden behind more visible and easily measured *doing* activities, using a model to explain how the virtual shop floor functions. The model is used to develop an understanding of the qualities of *useful* information and knowledge, explaining how knowledge can be tacitly held in people or explicitly represented in reports or objects.

The knowledge creation cycle – the new bottleneck

It should be clear by now that knowledge management involves a radical rethink of management focus. Managers are being asked to look at what lies behind the structures that corporations construct and the visible things that corporations do. Many, if not most, managers do not want to take on such a problematic area as knowledge and it is tempting to dismiss the topic entirely at this stage and get back to the security of managing things!

Information management continues to be seen as the primary purpose of intranets and systems in part because information can be counted in bytes and shipped in files. Managers can relate information management to other operational functions. Data is mined from databases just as orders can be picked from warehouses. The problem is that information management is treated as just another business logistics operation.

The logistics of the real shop floor are based on clear functional needs. Parts are moved to feed assembly lines. Consultants specify the number of days it will take to write up their findings. Goods are shipped to meet customer demand. Finance is transferred to enable transactions.

On the virtual shop floor, though, information is both the raw material and output of the knowledge processes. Its logistics need to be placed in a strategic context through knowledge management. Without a clear connection to its purpose on the virtual shop floor, information management becomes too concerned with information as a thing to be collected, stored and allocated for no clear purpose, comforting but pointless. It is no more efficient and effective than managing stock in ignorance of production plans and performance. The challenge and opportunity of the information and communication technology era is to exploit the sudden cornucopia of high quality information by managing the virtual shop floor itself.

Management has always concentrated on preventing, relieving and exploiting bottlenecks. After all, the scarce resource is the most valuable. It sets the upper limit on production. Careful control of widgets is no help when the assembly line has stopped for want of thing-a-ma-jigs. In the 1960's enormous mainframes were dedicated to processing data. The capacity to collect data grew so great that students took degrees and launched careers in data management. The management challenge was *'to find the nuggets of information concealed in the mountains of data.'* Information was the valuable bottleneck resource. Today, those *'nuggets'* have become mountains in their own right and the bottleneck is our capacity to use information. Information is consuming more and more management time. The space people need to think and learn has become the new bottleneck.

Knowledge management at Nortel Networks

Nortel Networks, the telecommunications and network solutions giant, became a knowledge manager when an employee survey revealed that its 55,000 staff felt unable to make proper use of the corporate intranet. And no wonder! By the end of 1997 it contained more than 1.5 million pages of data.

With the world total of electronically held data doubling every eighteen months, there must be many other organisations facing a similar decision.

The information bottleneck is such a big challenge because it is so hard to understand. In 1995, a consortium of seven local authorities in the midlands of England decided they could serve their constituencies more cost effectively if they combined their databases of education and training opportunities. Four years later, their plan is effectively dead, killed by long arguments about how to process too much information in too many forms. Their solution never lay in agreeing a common database, nor in any other technical agreement, but in resolving seven different sets of strategic objectives.

As long as they focus on the information, as opposed to finding a common purpose for it, their problem will remain. People are so conditioned to value information in its own right that they rarely consider how it is used. Yet information has no purpose unless it is connected by its users with their knowledge work.

Naïve notions of information and knowledge

Traditionally, in economic theory, possession of information is seen as the same as knowing what to do, and knowing what to do as the same as doing it. Adam Smith described a world in which labour, natural resources and capital were combined together and supplied to markets by purely rational capitalists using scientific principles. In the world of economic theory, all that differentiated entrepreneurs was the quantity of information that they possessed. Profits were gained by those with the most and best information, because it caused them to make the best decisions.

Yet, a moment's thought about entrepreneurs in the real world reveals the absurdity of imagining *rational* entrepreneurs making *the best* use of information as if their individual knowledge did not matter. Richard Branson used to stay up to party with staff in his first Virgin stores and is often seen serving as a cabin steward on trans-Atlantic Virgin flights. Dick Dukes used to take cases of beer around to operatives in the early days of ChemLawn[1]. Johnson and Johnson once flew the entire staff of a newly acquired English subsidiary to Wisconsin to bond with fellow employees and to strengthen corporate culture[2].

These are examples of emotional management, impossible to justify on purely rational grounds until afterwards, when the corporations have been seen to succeed[3].

It is odd how we cling to the theoretical model of rational decision-making, when it is so clearly ignored in our practices. Consider the case of the Harvard Business School MBA programme.

---

[1] Breakthroughs!

[2] I was unable to find anyone at Johnson & Johnson who remembered this event from the 1970's.

[3] If they were justifiable as purely rational management acts then, presumably, workforces everywhere would be swilling management-supplied beer or flying to global headquarters on planes served by airline MD's acting as flight attendants.

Why we value Harvard MBA's

The Harvard MBA is considered the best MBA programme in the world, and it is generally conceded that it attracts the best quality students. The Harvard MBA model is based on the preparation and presentation of case studies in classes. At the heart of the Harvard learning philosophy is an emphasis on debates based on different analyses of case studies.

If there were such a thing as uniquely best interpretations of information, one would expect less discussion as classes got better, because more students would get answers right. There would be no point in discussions once students had worked out that they all agreed with each other. In fact, the high status of the Harvard MBA reflects the very richness of classroom debates arising from different interpretations of the case studies. If there were such a thing as the right answer to a business problem, there would be no point in the Harvard model.

Knowledge in the shadows

Knowledge work has stayed in the shadows for so long because it is hidden behind other activities. When it took days, weeks, months or even years for problems and decisions to be communicated, there was a lot of time for the knowledge work to go on unnoticed. Captain Bligh, having recovered from the mutiny on the Bounty in 1789, was made Governor of Australia in 1805, where there was another mutiny. By the time the British government found out about it, and had got someone out to Australia to deal with it, the mutiny had been over for five years. The troops they immediately dispatched to Australia to put down the mutiny had nothing to do when they got there. A few years later, in 1815, General Andrew Jackson's American troops decisively defeated the

British in the Battle of New Orleans, neither side aware that the war had ended two weeks before. As late as 1919 there were no paved roads outside of the cities in all of the United States. It took a US Army convoy two months to cross the United States in a special test conducted *to see if it was physically possible.*

Consider the logistics of manufacturing as set out in the figure below. All of the real shop floor processes can take time and offer possibilities of delay. Employees are not physically doing their jobs when there are such delays, so it is natural to see such moments as wasted.

Logistics in manufacturing

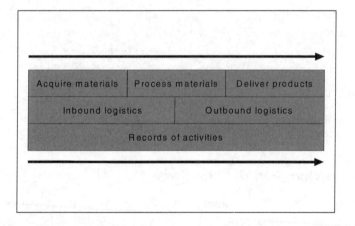

When it takes so long to do things, it is easy to overlook the time needed to know what to do and how to do it. The slowness of communication systems bought time for knowledge workers without us realising it.

Before e-mail, letters and memos really were *'in the post.'* Before computerised logistics monitoring and control, parts really were *'somewhere between here and Chicago.'* While waiting for others to do their jobs, people had time to think and to talk to each other about their own jobs. Their knowledge work took place hidden in the shadows of highly visible physical tasks.

Knowledge transfer despite management

I remember working on an assembly line twenty-five years ago. When the line was slow or stopped, workers were still required to look busy at their stations. To alleviate boredom at such times, skilled workers would trade places with their assistants and labourers. This allowed the less skilled to have a go at a time when their lack of experience would not interfere with the pace of production. It was the only training anyone got in that plant and raised the flexibility of operatives, but managers appeared not to understand that. Trading positions was called '*Hollywood*,' probably because we were acting at other people's jobs. Workers enjoyed it and foremen tolerated it in the hope that senior management would not notice, but foremen risked demotion or even dismissal if their lines were too obviously '*in Hollywood*'.

It was hard and dirty work and staff turnover was high. Line workers were regularly required to take on different roles due to absenteeism. *Hollywood* made role changes less disruptive to production and kept the line moving. Nowadays, we might praise the positive way that the shop floor shared its knowledge when production was slow or halted. Back then, learning and knowledge transfer were so little understood by senior management in that firm that they inadvertently sought to prevent it in the name of efficiency.

Knowledge in the sunlight

Long term preoccupation with the management of things and of productive tasks leaves organisations ill-prepared to cope with information and knowledge. The primary aim in the management of things and productive tasks is for greater speed and accuracy at lower cost. When tasks are repetitive and things are visible, such management is relatively straightforward, but information is used in ways that are neither visible nor repetitive.

Clearly, one of the first aims of knowledge management must be to bring knowledge out of the shadows and into the sunlight. Managers need to acknowledge that such work is happening and that it is more than the repetitive gathering and processing of information.

As the first knowledge management principle states, the value of information is defined by the people that receive it. If they believe it (it fits with their reality), employ it (it is useful) and share it (they can communicate it) then they will attach a higher value to it. For the Hewlett-Packard salesperson and the BT executive too much information has squeezed their time. If they could find a way to concentrate just on the messages that meant the most to them, and ignore the rest, they could give those messages *'the attention that they deserve.'*

One of the best illustrations of what this means comes from Dow Chemical, which has always managed its information as a portfolio of intellectual assets. In 1993 Dow set out to link its intellectual asset management with its business processes, that is, to become a knowledge manager. Initial motivation came from the discovery that more than half its library of 29,000 patents was lying unused. Over the past seven years, simply through tighter and more active management of its patent portfolio, Dow has achieved cost savings of more than $40 million and a five-fold increase in licence revenue to $125million annually. New patents are registered with specific business objectives, and the performance of intellectual assets is reviewed regularly.

Similarly, Pacific Bell has developed a system for measuring the value that information adds to processes, called business process auditing. With it, Pacific Bell seeks to better evaluate new processes, to better understand the worth of the information it collects and to better identify what should be collected.

IBM has reckoned to save millions of dollars and to have discovered new revenue streams by consolidating its marketing information into an inter-active *'Guide to Market Information'*, which covers internal and external sources and enables close communication between information owners and seekers. Despite generating more patents than any other corporation in the world, IBM had no system for their external exploitation in 1993. By the end of 1998 licences had earned more than $8 billion.

What these cases point towards is the place of the active and purposeful management of information in a comprehensive knowledge management strategy. The flow chart below sets out the knowledge process cycle in organisations. It shows the central function of the virtual shop floor, sharing is drawn as a cloud to emphasise its lack of precise definition and boundaries.

Knowledge sharing informs and accompanies the activities of the real shop floor. That is how knowledge work takes place in support of the pursuit of organisational objectives. The two cannot be separated in practice, because they are the two sides of the same coin. The virtual and real shop floors do not exist independently of each other.

The knowledge process cycle in organisations

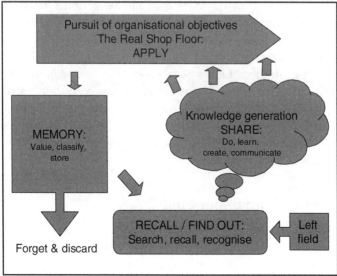

Knowledge enters the corporation through the interaction of people with the environment. Both by remembering lessons drawn from activities on the real shop floor and from their general life experiences (out of left field), employees acquire new ideas and insights. One of the best known examples of insights 'from left field' arose from choirmaster Arthur Fry's desire to mark places in his choir's hymn books. It was an essential factor in the development of post-it notes at 3M, where he worked as a chemist. He shared his choir's need with his colleagues and set in train investigations which led to the discovery of a new product with a massive market.

At the same time, the corporate memory cycle captures and recycles knowledge. The organisation stores in its memory what it has learned, recycling some and discarding the rest. Physicians, for example, keep records of patients to help treat them in the future. Those records can be combined with other records to enable medical researchers to gain insights into the nature and treatment of diseases. Multiple Sclerosis and Tourette's Syndrome both went unrecognised until the middle of the Victorian era because individual doctors saw too few cases to recognise them as diseases. Records had to be shared before the common patterns emerged.

All 'real' activities depend on the workings of the virtual shop floor. The information generated on the virtual shop floor enters corporate memory from which it can be recalled, applied and reviewed in future activities. At the same time, new information is being created within the organisation which further enriches the activity on the virtual shop floor. If the information management system is working efficiently, it both captures the current outcomes of the virtual shop floor and delivers relevant information back to it.

Learning from experience

Organisations must learn from new experiences and from memory to survive. Without new knowledge there can be no change and adaptation. Without memory, there can be no routines or linking narrative to give meaning. In people, this lack of narrative is a devastating illness. The personal tragedy of Altzheimer's disease is that it halts the coherence of its victims' lives by attacking memory. In organisations, memory is also essential to survival. It places new experiences into context and enables learned responses and routines, without which no corporation could survive long.

A matter of identity

Dr. Oliver Sachs is a neuropsychologist who has treated patients who have suffered brain damage[4]. He wrote the following about a Mr. Thompson, who lost his capacity to remember events at the very moment that they happen:

'*If we wish to know a man we ask "What is his story – his real, innermost story?" – for each of us is a biography... a singular narrative, which is constructed continually by, through and in us... Biologically, physiologically, we are not so different from each other; historically, as narratives – we are each of us unique.*

'*To be ourselves, we must **have** ourselves – possess, if need be repossess our life-stories... A man **needs** such a narrative, a continuous inner narrative, to maintain his identity, his self... For here is a man* [Mr Thompson] *who, in some sense, is desperate, in a frenzy. The world keeps disappearing, losing meaning, vanishing – and he must seek meaning, make meaning, in a desperate way, continually inventing, throwing bridges of meaning over abysses of meaninglessness, the chaos that yawns continually beneath him.*'

Oliver Sachs, *The Man who Mistook his Wife for a Hat*, Picador, London, 1985

---

[4] Some of Dr. Sachs' story is told in the Oscar-winning film, *Awakenings*, in which he is portrayed by Robin Williams.

Just as our memory places new experience in context, so new experience keeps memories relevant. Organisations need to learn from new experiences in order not to trap themselves in dated technologies, products or strategies. At the same time, they need the memory of previous experience in order not to be blown away by new changes in their environment.

The general retail sector is a rich source of long-lived corporations that, having achieved excellence, stopped learning new things and so brought about their own downfall. In America, Sears Roebuck was the unsurpassed leader in general retailing and the innovator which created the popular credit card market throughout the 1960's and 1970's. In Great Britain, Marks and Spencer (M & S) set the European standard for departmental store quality in the 1980's.

Both Sears and M&S built their dominant market positions on experience and learning that dates back to Victorian times. Having achieved their pinnacles, both concentrated on fulfilling their visions of excellence, not responding to signals from the market that *it* was changing *its* vision of excellence. By the 1980's Sears had lost its position in the credit sector to Visa and others, and its general retailing position to the likes of Wal-Mart and the Gap – fast-moving competitors who responded to market changes that Sears either missed or ignored. M&S was toppled by its long tradition of refusing to accept credit cards and its inability to change its clothing lines as rapidly as specialist high street clothing retailers like Next, River Island, French Connection and the Gap (again). The conservative M&S strategy of entering markets later but with higher quality is inappropriate when fashions change so fast that 'later' is too late.

One of the most influential management trends of the last decade, Business Process Re-engineering (BPR), has been widely misapplied in a way that encourages corporations to stop learning. At the heart of BPR is the notion that employees have already learned the best ways to do things. Many BPR initiatives have exploited corporate memory cycles to achieve enormous and immediate efficiency gains and cost savings. Unfortunately, the many redundancies that have accompanied the efficiency gains have damaged the capacity of corporations to learn and change in the future. Too much knowledge has left the firms because it was carried in the minds of redundant workers, while those who remain are too busy to find the time to reflect on what they do or to explore creative possibilities.

A key sign of corporate inability to learn is being most efficient at something the market no longer requires. When Henry Ford offered his customers any coloured car, *'so long as it's black'*, he was demonstrating an inability to learn from new experience. Marks and Spencer's crown as the leading 1980's-style general retailer is a poor one to carry into the next millennium, precisely because the lessons of a decade of market changes have not been learned.

The virtual shop floor in action

Geoff Smith, knowledge transformation manager at Cap Gemini UK, makes the distinction between data-rich companies, which are able to collect and record relevant data, and knowledge-driven enterprises that are able to identify, encourage and exploit knowledge to achieve corporate ends. He contrasts the IT-oriented and knowledge-based views of knowledge management. *'With the support of knowledge a business can wade through the morass of information and data.'*

He identifies three forces that link knowledge and information and presents them as questions:

- *What knowledge do I need to support decisions and core competences in my business?*
- *What sources of intelligence and insight help to support and develop my knowledge?*
- *What information and data are available to prove the value of my knowledge and to help generate new insights?*

As was explained earlier, information has to have certain qualities before it can be accepted by users. These are that it must be:

- Grounded in reality as we understand it. Otherwise we cannot accept it.
- Useful. If it has no utility to its possessor, it has no point and will be forgotten.
- Communicable to others. Otherwise it cannot be confirmed and shared.

The virtual shop floor is where these qualities are continually being tested. The knowledge work that takes place, as we do things, learn, share, debate and create, will lead us to add new information to our corporate memory and revise or reject old information in it. At the heart of the virtual shop floor there is a continuous process of justifying beliefs.

Consider a project team set up two decades ago by a major energy corporation to build power plants in the former Soviet Union. As the team worked together, its members learned all sorts of things about turbines, teamwork, global projects in general and Soviet projects in particular. Their reports were rich in useful information that reflected their deep and up-to-date knowledge. Project members were consulted and their reports read by colleagues. Their knowledge was a living and changing thing, because their reports, presentations and conversations were continually being challenged, added to and reapplied by them and their colleagues.

Eventually though, the project team broke up and their knowledge began to fade. The engineers moved on to other projects, left the firm and forgot. No apparent loss to the corporation, because the collapse of the Soviet Union appeared to spell the end for that market. New technologies and new projects in different countries came up. The information in their reports referred to out-dated computer languages, methods, economic questions and other issues that were no longer useful or even comprehensible to modern readers. As the individuals, the team and the organisation moved on to other concerns, their knowledge lost its currency. The richness of the corporate knowledge gained from the project diminished and the information that remained in corporate reports and databases progressively lost meaning and usefulness.

Eventually all that remained was data that no one could use. It had become:

- Ungrounded – the corporation no longer does those sorts of projects.
- Unpragmatic – the technology is out-of-date. The tools are no longer used.
- Incommunicable – the records sit in inaccessible files and use the language of technologies that are no longer used or understood.
- Uncontested – no thought is given to the lessons learned. They are either believed and applied without question or dismissed without consideration.

All they had learned was forgotten, because no one had a use for it. The lost knowledge ended up costing the corporation millions though, because recently, when Russian operators of the now-aged plants wanted to refurbish them, they turned to the original builders. Alas, their memory had let them down. They still had much of the vital information in the form of original plans and reports, but lacked the knowledge to bring out its value. They could not respond positively and the contract was lost.

Chun Wei Choo, a professor at the University of Toronto, puts it best[5]: '*It is the individual who breathes meaning and energy into bloodless information.*' According to Professor Choo, individuals construct meanings depending on their individual knowledge and situation. What we attach meaning to is influenced by the social groups to which we belong.

One of the important factors will be the main purpose of a group, for example, recipes will be valuable information to a restaurant company. Another will be the ruling social attitudes of a group, qualitative information may be rejected by a finance department which prefers to deal with quantitative data.

---

[5] Chun Wei Choo, *The Knowing Organization*, Sage, London, 1998.

Tacit and explicit knowledge

In the model of the organisational knowledge process cycle we were deliberately vague about what actually happens on the virtual shop floor, because so many different processes are possible in the doing, learning, sharing and creating that generates knowledge.

Knowledge is held either tacitly or explicitly.

Tacit knowledge is what individuals know. It is called tacit because it is personally held and may not even be recognised as knowledge by its holder. Tacit knowledge includes subjective know-how, insights and intuitions. It is a dynamic flow, ever-changing with the experience of its possessor. A salesman, for instance, continually alters his tacit knowledge of customers, sales pitches and products as he goes about his job.

Explicit knowledge, on the other hand, is formally held in the form of reports, equations, formulae, specifications and the like. It is easily transmitted between individuals and groups. The formal capture of explicit knowledge fixes it. However, the originator's tacit knowledge may change, the explicit report, film or programme remains as a snapshot of what the tacit knowledge was at the moment it was captured.

In the figure opposite Nonaka and Takeuchi classify the four different ways in which knowledge is converted/developed:

1. Socialisation – the sharing of tacit knowledge between individuals.
2. Externalisation – where tacit knowledge is made explicit.
3. Combination – which involves the combination of two or more pieces of explicit knowledge to make up another piece of explicit knowledge.
4. Internalisation – transforming explicit knowledge into tacit knowledge.

Knowledge conversion/development

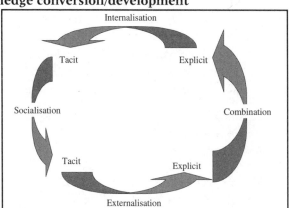

Internalisation

Tacit   Explicit

Socialisation   Combination

Tacit   Explicit

Externalisation

Nonaka and Takeuchi, 1996.

1. Socialisation

The transfer of tacit knowledge between people (tactit to tacit) is a social process. A trainee watches a skilled worker to learn how the job is done. An intern assists a qualified surgeon. He both observes her actions and listens to her talk. After a sales meeting, sales people gather in the pub to trade 'war stories' about sales pitches and difficult customers. Tacit knowledge lacks form because it is continually changing in people's heads and as it is transferred between people.

2. Externalisation

Making tacit knowledge explicit is a process of externalisation. The instructional articles in golf magazines about 'Tiger Woods' golfing secrets' are examples of externalisation. In business, we may externalise tacit knowledge by writing a report, filming an activity or developing a CADCAM programme. Once tacit knowledge has been made explicit, it is fixed as information.

It can be difficult or even impossible to make knowledge explicit. We can be so familiar with tacit knowledge that we 'forget' that we know it, so our explicit representations may leave out important parts of which we are unconscious. When that happens, it is hard to find words or representations that carry meaning to our intended audience. Sports stars are often dismissed as dim-witted 'jocks' because they are notoriously unable to put into appropriate words the grace and physical intelligence of their game-winning plays. Brilliant corporate operational performers often fail in management roles because they are unable to externalise the tacit basis of their excellence.

As easy as falling off a bike

IBM's John Blackwell used to open presentations by asking his audience to imagine how they could make the gift of a bicycle to 'little nine year-old Johnny' more complete. He suggested, *'Why don't we put our heads together and write a manual for him so he doesn't have to go through all the pain and difficulty that usually accompanies learning to ride a bike?'*

It always got a good laugh and led nicely into his key point. Some knowledge can only be tacit. Nobody learns to ride a bike from an instruction manual.

3. Combination

Explicit knowledge can be combined to make more explicit knowledge. Examples of combination include automatically generated regional sales reports and process integration systems. They save time and effort by digesting and repackaging material into more useful forms.

The capacity to combine explicit knowledge well brings enormous efficiency benefits to organisations. This is because the tacit knowledge and thinking on which the combination process depends has already been done and captured. It does carry a risk, though. The reasoning behind externalised knowledge is likely to be taken for granted and forgotten once the externalisation and combination processes are in place. Automated processes can become invisible. Most organisations are full of examples of automatically generated reports which are produced because the system is set up to produce them for reasons which are no longer entirely clear.

4. Internalisation

Lastly, there is internalisation. This is where explicit knowledge is turned back into tacit knowledge. Information only has value if there is the knowledge to give it meaning. When we internalise explicit knowledge, we are valuing the explicitly-presented knowledge of others enough to think about it and use it ourselves. Think of the e-mails and reports that you trash without reading. They have failed to get through your mental filter.

From tacit to explicit and back again

I began thinking about writing this book about two years ago. I spent a long time talking with a close colleague and friend, John Kawalek, and with others, about knowledge management. I was deepening my tacit understanding through a process of socialisation. This book is a source of explicit knowledge derived from my tacit knowledge. In it I have tried to externalise my tacit knowledge.

Someone may care to put this explicit representation of my knowledge through another piece of explicit knowledge, a linguistic analysis programme, to see whether or not the book was really written by William Shakespeare or a team of chimpanzees. That would be an example of combining the explicit knowledge in the book with the explicit knowledge in the programme.

As you read, you will be reshaping your knowledge by internalising the information that I have supplied, but it will be your internalised knowledge and not mine. So, my explicit knowledge will influence your tacit knowledge.

Nonaka and Takeuchi criticise American management for being too preoccupied with explicit knowledge. They point out that explicit knowledge is easier to control and transmit, because it is formal and fixed. Explicit knowledge is most useful in situations that call for repetition and increasing efficiency. The classic exploiter of explicit knowledge was Henry Ford, who made the skills and knowledge of automobile manufacture explicit. His assembly lines were not just a means of producing cars. They were an explicit representation of how to produce cars according to the Ford Motor Company.

The great advantage of explicit knowledge combination is that it takes pressure off knowledge workers by automatically generating new knowledge, saving human time and effort. Unfortunately, once we make knowledge explicit, it becomes 'official' and hard to shift. Think about the automatic reports that are generated by corporate information systems. They can be useful sources of explicit knowledge, but they can only ever supply knowledge within the framework set out by the system's designers.

Explicit knowledge does not nurture creativity or support change. For that you need the ever-changing tacit knowledge of people who are experiencing the environment. We need to make knowledge explicit in order to help the whole organisation benefit from it and to ease the knowledge bottleneck, but we need to continuously challenge explicit knowledge with new tacit outputs from the virtual shop floor. Nonaka and Takeuchi argue that the secret of Japanese corporate success lies in their ability to innovate, and that their creativity is due to their cultural capacity to continuously challenge established explicit knowledge with new tacit knowledge. They quote the case of a researcher at Matsushita who apprenticed herself to a master breadmaker in order to capture his tacit knowledge of how to knead bread. Matsushita designed a new breadmaking machine that incorporated what she had learned.

The knowledge bottleneck

Information and data are both the material inputs used on the virtual shop floor (literally, food for thought) and the outputs that are produced there. Knowledge workers employ data and information as part of the doing, sharing, creating and learning which goes into knowledge work. In so doing, they create more information and data. Thus, as we produce knowledge, much of it becomes part of our information resource. That might suggest that knowledge management could be left to the information managers. In most cases, the combination of explicit knowledge is left to them.

The knowledge management challenge, though, is that too much information on too many potentially important subjects is now available. The volume of knowledge made explicit and accessible through intranets and the Internet is almost infinite. The virtual shop floor, like any other workspace, can become clogged with too much material. The capacity to inform can overpower the capacity to be informed.

One of the criticisms of classroom training is that it is so inefficient that, on average, only about 20% of what is taught is actually learned. Most of us can remember how we crammed for exams at school or university, only to forget the lot almost as soon as the exams were finished. It had served its purpose and was discarded. Information management does not address the challenge raised by the fact that information is only valuable if there is a purpose to give it meaning. As recently as five years ago, a market research consultant in Sheffield told me that he advised new entrepreneurs to *'go out and find out everything you can about the market. Even if it seems irrelevant, collect it, just in case.'* Today, the poor entrepreneur would be in trouble trying to digest *'everything you can find out about the market.'* Thanks to information and communications technology, the table is piled too high with food for thought.

The organisation that concentrates attention on information management is not giving adequate attention to the purpose of information. It is trying to manage the inputs and outputs of knowledge work without managing the processes, like a farmer who buys a dairy herd, hay and bottles, then sits back to wait for all the milk. It will not happen, or if it does, the farmer will not appreciate just how dependent he is on the good will and efforts of some extremely talented cows. The organisation that explicitly seeks to manage knowledge processes must uncover the hidden part of the virtual shop floor.

This was brought home recently when I reviewed a set of interviews of key staff at a global industrial information provider which was having trouble persuading employees to use its intranet. In the first five transcripts there were five different examples of knowledge bottlenecks:

- A salesman in Portugal who had developed a technical database with a colleague over the Internet to help him solve client problems. *'They depend on me. My credibility is on the line.'* Yet management knows nothing about it. It is the private property of the two salesmen, a positive example of explicit knowledge that could benefit all sales staff instead of just two.
- A legal assistant who maintains the contract forms and status database using the corporate intranet, but observes, *'I believe I am the only one who has access.* [It's] *...not used a great deal.'* The assistant's knowledge of contract forms and of their status is being made explicit on the intranet for no one's benefit, not even her own.
- A senior manager who thinks *'e-mail, although it's a great concept, ... actually doesn't particularly help... More often than not you can usually pick up key issues in the corridor, while you're getting coffee. It's a cliché, but everyone knows it to be true. Because people are less inhibited in that situation and they tend to discuss more freely what is going on.'* Clear anecdotal evidence that official communication channels are not trusted. How can the board be confident that its messages are getting across, when casual and uncertain gossip is the most trusted medium? What are employees making of official communications?

- A technology development manager who is *'getting an external programmer to create an information system. An intranet is not good enough…'* This is an example of wasteful duplication of effort and costs. When another formal information system is set up alongside the official formal system there has to be something wrong. This is a good illustration of how the virtual shop floor and the information system can become disconnected.

- An administrative assistant who sends out bulky paper updates of guidelines on product pricing, specifications, codings and so on *'…to all head people in the local offices. They then distribute and copy it to people in their areas. It's quite time consuming… I post the majority and some I fax, but e-mail, not really… I have to call them to check that they have received their updates.'* The possibilities for customer dissatisfaction at slow and inaccurate service are just enormous.

The five transcripts set the tone of all the others, revealing an equal mix of wasted effort and under-exploited creativity on the virtual shop floor costing untold millions in actual losses and missed opportunities. Yet the corporation has opted to put in place an entirely new intranet to serve a virtual shop floor of which management remains ignorant. Knowledge management offers the corporation an opportunity to support and direct the abilities and efforts of its employees to improve the benefits it gains from their knowledge, but at the moment, it is choosing to change the information system without addressing the central question of the way it is used and the value to the corporation of that use.

In effect, management is hoping that appropriate knowledge will be generated and effectively shared through the new information system. No one is addressing the central questions posed by the virtual shop floor. How do its processes contribute to corporate performance, and how can they be improved? That brings us to the *second and final principle*.

Second principle: Knowledge management is primarily the management of the processes that generate knowledge, rather than the management of knowledge itself.

Conclusion – the management challenge of knowledge creation

The value of information lies in how it is used. Information collected for its own sake or because some manager has decided it is important swiftly clogs up systems. Information management adds value when the system supports and encourages the flow of the information that knowledge workers need and use and discourages the flow of information that they do not need and use.

In many ways, the very name 'knowledge management' is misleading, because it encourages managers to think of knowledge as an explicit thing. Such an approach reduces knowledge management to information management and is doomed to fail.

The real management challenge of knowledge is to make organisations better at learning, creating and sharing. It requires an understanding of how the virtual shop floor operates in order to improve its efficiency and effectiveness in support of organisational objectives.

When employees feel unable to share lessons that they have learned, when opportunities to innovate are consistently missed, or when people are regularly unable to collaborate in ways that could benefit the organisation, then these are failures of process that effective management ought to be able to prevent.

Second principle: Knowledge management is primarily the management of the processes that generate knowledge, rather than the management of knowledge itself.

4

Why knowledge management now?

Introduction

An obvious question to ask of the advocates of knowledge management is, why now? If it is such an obvious piece of managerial good sense, wasn't it just as good sense back in 1900 or 1950?

This chapter considers how changes in the business environment have brought knowledge management to the fore now. *Globalisation* and the *information technology revolution* are so familiar to us that it is sometimes easy to overlook just how radically they are altering the business environment. They are at the heart of the rise of knowledge management and are the primary focus of this chapter.

The latest hot topic?

We start this chapter with two examples of knowledge management. Both incorporate principles that are anything but earth-shakingly new. Tesco, the UK supermarket chain, collects and uses customer knowledge in a focused way to increase customer satisfaction and loyalty. US West tapped into the knowledge of its sales people to improve a process.

Two short cases

A.   A friend, Rupert Dale, does not eat red meat. When he shops at the Tesco supermarket chain they track his purchases through his Tesco Club Card. Periodically they send him special offer coupons. In 1998 these included red meat offers. By early 1999 he noticed that Tesco was only sending coupons that reflected his actual purchasing pattern. He no longer gets red meat coupons, and he likes shopping at Tesco.

B.   In 1997, when US West, the American telecommunications corporation, analysed sales of one of its most complex products, its Centrex-21 system, it discovered that sales people were spending an average of two hours writing orders and making numerous errors, which drove up costs, delayed order completion and annoyed customers. The solution was to gather information from a range of sales representatives and form a corporate rule base for Centrex-21 orders. The corporate intranet was employed to ensure that the new rule base was applied universally. US West was able to reduce order writing time by 90%, eliminate the production backlog, related errors and rework. Customers and sales reps were happier; order profitability rose and sales increased.

What *is* new is the scale of what corporations can do to manage their knowledge and the speed with which they can do it. If Tesco's success with its Club Card were a one-off, Tesco's competition could copy it and relax, but Tesco is doing much more. Club Card information now automatically alters store stocking and re-ordering operations. More than that, it connects the whole of Tesco's internal processes with the customer, by making accurate and current customer information part of the intelligence that informs every decision.

Similarly, if US West had merely stumbled on a new tool for order writing its competitors would only have to copy it; but what if the corporation has found a different way of thinking about its business processes? In that case, the improved order writing for Centrex-21 will be just one application of a new philosophy and competitors will have to plan for more competitive changes from US West. If they want to stay competitive, they will have to put in place their own global villages. Here are a set of quotes from Peter Briggs of US West:

'A systematic view... transcends work cell boundaries and helps people come to a shared mental model of the situation...'

'The study also brought to the conscious level the idea that "information about the network is as important as the network itself".'

'... in an organisation where knowledge management is not an overt cultural concern, knowledge assets can be damaged inadvertently... At US West we are evolving quickly towards a culture that expects to produce knowledge and to learn as an integral part of the job.'

What the two cases and the quotes suggest is a profound philosophical development. US West and Tesco do not mind if competitors seek to copy what they do, because they see their advantage deriving from what they know, something which cannot be duplicated. Yet, if knowledge management does offer so many advantages why has it waited until now to appear? The past two decades have been ones of almost frantic change, with 'management fads' appearing and being replaced with bewildering rapidity. Many managers tell us that knowledge management is no more than today's hot topic. In the rest of this chapter we consider *why knowledge management now?*

A different business environment

Practically everywhere I go, I hear that doing business is more difficult than it used to be. Claims such as the following are typical[1]:

---

[1] M. J. Kiernan, *Get Innovative or Get Dead!*, Century, London, 1995.

'Markets are infinitely more complicated, turbulent and far-flung, and competitors can come at you from anywhere and at any time.'

Where there used to be three competitors, now there are twenty (who we know about). Customers have more options, and they know it. Unforeseen innovations can make the securest of markets vulnerable at a stroke. Giants like Netscape and Amazon.com emerge overnight, while others depart as quickly. Was it less than fifteen years ago that Digital stood shoulder to shoulder with IBM, a paragon of *excellence* for all the world to admire?

There are a number of closely related causes at work:

- The world is a simpler place to do business in than it used to be!
- Lean and fit organisations may do things better, but they are not necessarily better at changing what they do.
- Knowledge workers are powerful and valuable people who are reviewing their roles as employees.
- Customers manage knowledge.

Some of these factors are obvious, but others are not, and the implications of all of them are worth exploring.

The world is a simpler place to do business in than it used to be!

How has competition changed in the past decade? There are more competitors, lower barriers to entry, fewer protected markets and the customer is becoming increasingly powerful. Certainly these developments make the business environment *look* more complex, but they are actually symptoms of its growing simplicity. The fluidity of markets and business practices that are associated with globalisation did not happen in the past because they were not possible or were not forced by the pressure of competition.

Previously unthinkable business developments are now the norm. More than ever before, the world economy is coming closer together. Companies compete as barriers between product and service markets, and between national markets, melt away. The challenge of management is made harder because there is less certainty and less stability.

A case of disappearing barriers to competition

In 1990, British Gas was in the gas industry, Scottish Electricity was an electricity utility and British Telecom was a telephone company. They were separate utility sector oligopolists and regional monopolists in their various fields, exploiting apparently unrelated markets through separate channels and linking them to businesses and homes. Today they compete and co-operate in previously unimagined ways in what might be called mega-markets, a vast, rapidly changing environmental response to deregulation, privatisation, technological advances and trade liberalisation. Their previously specialised channels of pipes, electricity and telephone lines and service networks are now seen to be wonderfully flexible and intimately related sources of competitive advantage.

In 1990 British Gas produced and distributed only gas and gas appliances. By 1999, its trading arm, Centrica, marketed gas and electricity to consumers who could pay via its aggressively marketed Goldfish credit card, the fastest growing UK credit card scheme in 1997. We could even guard our homes with British Gas home insurance and security system service.

In addition, British Gas is one of more than 150 competitors now crowding the telecommunications industry where just thirteen years before there was only British Telecom. They rub shoulders with Sky, building on its satellite television success, the water utility Compagnie Generale des Eaux, numerous cable television companies, Railtrack (the privatised owner of the British railway network) and aggressively competitive electricity suppliers and distributors like United Utilities and Yorkshire Electricity.

To complete the circle, electricity generators PowerGen and Hydro-electric of Scotland are buying gas fields. Meanwhile the British Automobile Association was taken over by Centrica in 1999. Previously unimaginable connections are being made between industries and markets as network-based companies have come to recognise that they operate what London's *Financial Times* calls '*marketing highways*' into homes and businesses.

Why is the global business environment less complicated than it used to be? The key is communication. There is now so much accessible information that there are few markets where companies can keep out competitors just by controlling information. Satellite television, for instance, has raised the overwhelming dominance of English as the world business language to a point where no significant market is closed to English speakers. On the day in 1999 that Sheffield Business School advertised its new Master of Science degree in Knowledge Management and Consultancy, its very first enquiry was an e-mail from Argentina. By the end of the day, enquiries from the rest of the world outnumbered British ones by two to one. All were in English.

The capacity to speak the same language is augmented by the speed of communication. The Internet ensures that advantages of geographical location are minimised. German luxury car-maker Mercedes-Benz produces customised cars in response to American customers directly linked to their German plants from American showrooms. US giant General Motors relocated its international division headquarters from Switzerland back to Detroit in 1998. There is no longer any perceived advantage in placing managers physically close to markets.

At the same time, political and cultural barriers to doing business are lessening. The European Union is growing both closer and larger. The six nation European Common Market of 1959 has become the fifteen member European Union in just forty years, while communism's Iron Curtain has been entirely swept aside. Shanghai University is now producing MBA-qualified managers to meet the growing demand for them in the People's Republic of China, in direct competition with American, British and Australian universities, which all offer MBA study to students based in China. The University of Chicago's Business School has even opened a campus in Singapore to serve the Pacific Rim market.

Thirty years ago, only the dollar, yen and a few European currencies were freely exchanged. Foreign markets were exotic and mysterious places. There was no CNN on the television.

Foreign languages, standards and cultures were minefields for the unwary. Export deals required complex and exact form-filling. Such difficulties served as barriers to global commerce. On my first ever export deal, the Colombian customer simply accepted the product and never paid the invoice or replied to my letters. On my next deal, foreign exchange controls cost my company most of the profit margin. It was a steep learning curve. Good thing I was the boss!

Business activities that used to be so difficult because the world was complicated are now happening because it is less so. Formal trade restrictions, such as exchange controls, tariffs and so on, have been lessened or removed, while the barriers of language, culture and physical distance have been lessened by technology.

A simpler world

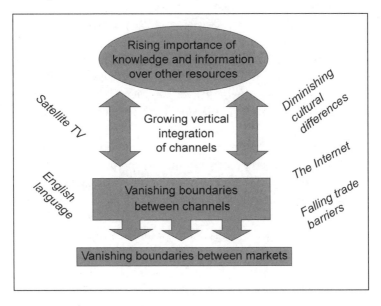

Where once information was scarce and unevenly distributed, now it is plentiful and far more accessible. This has thrown attention onto how information is used, that is, the processes of knowledge. Companies that used to have a local or national advantage are starting to manage knowledge because they have to in order to stay ahead. Global competitors have access to just as much good quality information and an ever-improving capacity to exploit it.

Lean and fit organisations may do things better, but they are not necessarily better at changing what they do

The 1980's and 1990's have been the decades of downsizing, de-layering and business process re-engineering. Urged on by Tom Peters, Michael Hammer, James Champy and other gurus of BPR, corporations have stripped out layers of middle management. Hammer and Champy explicitly told managers to forget previous methods[2]. '*How people and companies did things yesterday doesn't matter to the business re-engineer.*' Job losses in middle management were '*one of the prices companies paid*' for growth.

The aim of all this restructuring and downsizing was a heroic corporate tiger, lean and fit. James Martin described it best in his book *Cybercorp*[3]: The successful modern competitor is '*a creature in the jungle stalking its prey... constantly alert. It monitors its environment in real time and can make immediate adjustments... It can suddenly move at great speed when it needs to... the survivor in the corporate jungle – the cybercorp.*'

The problem with the company-as-jungle-beast is that it is built on a false metaphor. Certainly, corporations need to be efficient at what they do today or they will not see tomorrow, but they also need to be flexible enough to change in response to what tomorrow may bring. Efficiency requires fewer and more focused people, but flexibility requires more people who are less focused and can notice and explore new ideas and possibilities. Tigers spend about twenty hours per day sleeping or resting, being inefficient, so they can be highly effective when they need to be.

---

[2] Hammer and Champy, p. 2.
[3] James Martin, *Cybercorp*, McGraw-Hill, London, 1996.

The late Jerry Junkins was CEO at Texas Instruments when he uttered the famous lament, '*If we only knew what we know at TI*[4].' Business Process Re-engineering is seen by many as having failed because the middle managers who were sacrificed to raise efficiency took their unrecognised knowledge with them. Downsized corporations lost much of their capacity to change and stay effective.

When an organisation is drawing on the knowledge of fewer people (after all the downsizing and de-layering) who are already working harder and in a more focused way (after re-engineering), it cannot simply trust that the knowledge it needs is there and will emerge when required. Some people have gone and those remaining are too busy to give new information their attention.

The Patricia Seybold Group of Boston, Massachusetts, uses the term '*to Amazon*' an industry. That is when a brand new company '*that is not hampered by current industrial practices invents a whole new way of doing business.*' For the short-sighted manager, the risk of being '*Amazoned*' is just another 'screwdriver' problem. If the corporation is not as innovative as its competitors, something is not working, so find the right tool and fix it. But such an approach ignores the fundamental nature of innovation. When something really new happens, you may have to throw out the whole toolbox and design afresh. Anthony O'Shea, a post-graduate student at Sunderland University, writes[5]: '*There cannot be a "best practice" model for product innovation.*' He argues that '*being innovative*' is a way of seeing the world. Managers who depend on one way to innovate will not see the innovative potential of other ways. We can learn from others' experience of innovation, but we cannot use them as benchmarks to copy.

Conrad Thompson, a senior knowledge management consultant at IBM, agrees with O'Shea. He is rarely asked by clients to

---

[4] I have since heard the same quote credited to a number of other sources, but Jerry Junkins was the first that I came across, so he gets the credit here.

[5] Anthony O'Shea, 'Innovation and product development and Pierre Bourdieu's theory of habitus, capital and field.' Paper delivered to the First International Conference in Critical Management, Manchester Business School, 7–9 July 1999.

introduce them to knowledge management. They ask him how they can become more innovative and effective. He argues that knowledge management is necessary for organisations that have to be innovative at the same time as they are raising efficiency. Corporations are looking to manage knowledge because they need to compete efficiently against today's competitors at the same time as they search out tomorrow's competitors and markets.

Knowledge workers are powerful and valuable people who are reviewing their roles as employees

We have already met the old corporate motto '*Our people are our most valuable assets.*' The fact that it is almost always ignored does not disguise its truth. As other resources become less protectable and more easily duplicated, people really are becoming the most important resource, because of their knowledge capacities. This means that employees have to be managed more carefully, so they stay as long as they are needed. It also means that employees have to be handled more effectively, so the organisation gets full benefit from their employment.

Whatever other assets the corporation may own, it is the employees who own their personal tacit knowledge and abilities. If they leave, they take their knowledge with them. If a nurse quits a hospital she may have to give back the thermometer and the bedpan, but she will take away all the skills and knowledge she has. As early as 1964, Marshall McLuhan not only predicted how the information age would change work, but recognised the power and independence it would give to workers.

'*Men are suddenly nomadic gatherers of knowledge, nomadic as never before, informed as never before, free from fragmentary specialism as never before.*'

The era of downsizing and BPR was notable for the reckless disregard for employee knowledge urged on managers. For the advocates of BPR, the past and, by implication, all its lessons, need to be forgotten. That is one reason why so many people were made redundant. In BPR all that matters is the newly re-engineered process and the people who are needed to operationalise it. When the *'nomads'* were told to pack their camels and hit the desert, they took their knowledge with them. Their employers, never having evaluated or managed that knowledge, did not recognise what they were losing until too late.

At Ernst & Young in 1998...

It cost approximately £100,000 to train and qualify a chartered accountant.

The average qualified accountant left within two years of qualifying.

The opportunity cost of a departed qualified accountant was around £80,000 in the first year after departure.

Barry Leskin, UK Head of HR, Ernst & Young, 1998

In March of 1998 I was asked to chair a business seminar in London and present a paper with John Kawalek, the systems expert, on the problem of 'employee churn'. Attendees were there in order to discuss how they could better hold onto their key workers. At the conference, a CEO from a Belgian software developer described how a recent take-over of a promising American software house went disastrously wrong after the key engineers all left. *'We have their offices, their products and their customers, but we have lost the main reason for investing in the business in the first place!'*

Lloyds TSB has developed a model to identify the knowledge of leavers and reasons for leaving. Managers want to know if important knowledge holders are going and why, so the bank can prevent serious knowledge loss in future. The likely value of the knowledge held by each type of employee has been assessed so that managers are alert to the implications of their departure for Lloyds TSB's knowledge base.

Lloyds TSB Staff Turnover Model

	Type A Voluntary turnover of staff	Type B Involuntary turnover of staff
High value	• Inadequate selection process for redundancy (voluntarily losing key workers and knowledge)	• Retention problem (involuntary loss of key workers)
Low value	• Dismissal or redundancy (low knowledge loss)	• Career development and guidance (either to raise value and prospects of worker or to make smoother departure)

In effect, Lloyds TSB is looking at employee retention as an aspect of knowledge management. When an employee is lost to the company, the loss is classified as Type A (voluntarily allowed to go) or Type B (involuntarily lost). Only the Type A loss of a low value employee is not a matter for concern. The Type A loss of a high value worker is a redundancy process failure, because such workers should be identified and protected. Type B employee losses are management failures, whatever the value of the worker. Key workers should want to stay and low value workers should be able to raise their capacity to contribute through employee development or to depart via the less disruptive Type A route.

The advantage of the process to Lloyds TSB is that it starts from the premise that employees should be evaluated in terms of the value of their capacity to contribute rather than their salary cost. Employees possess knowledge, receive training and have experience which may have been expensively purchased by their employer. The Lloyds TSB model demonstrates an awareness by management not only that high value people may choose to leave the organisation, but that the organisation can and does inadvertently get rid of such people voluntarily.

Customers manage knowledge

The last reason why knowledge management is necessary is the most important of all. Customers manage knowledge. More than that, they are getting better at it all the time. It is not just corporate customers. Final consumers have never been more aware of their options as customers and their rights as consumers.

In Great Britain, for example, the largest single retailer of wine and beer is France. Rather than pay tax-inflated British prices, more than 15% of purchasers cross the English Channel. A growing number travel to Holland or Belgium to buy their cars at a price discount of between 5% and 20%. The reason that they know to do so is that they communicate with each other more widely than ever before. Practically the whole of the British telephone betting industry has relocated or threatened to relocate overseas in response to tax differences. Victor Chandler's telephone call centre, for example, serves the British market from Gibraltar.

There are consumer reports on practically every product or market. Internet film review forums are claimed to have cost hundreds of millions by spreading bad reviews about films even before they are formally released. However, a student film that cost less than $50,000 to make, *The Blair Witch Project*, attracted good reviews from film buffs on the Internet. The major studios were forced to watch in fear and hope as the film went on to gross over $120 million in revenue.

The lessons from *The Blair Witch Project* are staggering. Its success was entirely controlled by consumers, *who chose to market it themselves*. As customers learn more, so corporations must develop their knowledge just to keep up.

There is almost no significant product or company that does not inspire an Internet-enabled independent forum. This is Oracle's Rick Powles quoted in *The Sunday Times* of 13 June 1999:

'We can have access to products from around the world without stepping out of our back door. We also have lots of opportunity for comparative shopping. Even if we don't buy things off the Web, we can check the prices

there and see how well they compare with the High Street... customer expectations are growing higher than ever at a time when margins are falling and response times have to be shorter. You have to move more quickly and smartly on lower margins all the time.'

The lesson is simple: the more that customers know, the more corporations must know to attract and keep them. A consumer will regard an individual purchase as important in a different way to the way the supplier will attach importance to one of many sales. Their focus is on the experience of buying, possessing and using an individual item. They share their knowledge in pubs, magazines, on the Internet and anywhere else much more spontaneously and creatively than organisations can. This is because their motivations are so different. They broadcast their satisfaction when they are happy with a purchase, and are even louder when it disappoints. Unlike a company disappointed by, say, a financial management system, there are no political or commercial reasons for a family to hide its disappointment when its shirts don't come out whiter than white, or they can believe it isn't butter. They tell their friends and neighbours what they have learned. Thanks to the Internet, they have a lot of friends and neighbours.

As they share knowledge, customers become increasingly powerful and proactive. In the 1970's and 1980's both Ford and General Motors chose to disregard growing public belief that popular models, Ford's Pinto and GM's 'C' and 'K' style pick-up trucks, were vulnerable to fire due to engineering faults. In 1999, the mere possibility of defects in automobiles regularly leads to manufacturer recalls of hundreds of thousands of cars.

Improved communications make it easy for previously isolated individual customers to become causes, and even crusades. Minority interests gain critical mass. Nearly every major corporation has inspired an anti-homepage where negative information about it and its products can be found. In 1999 a report of possible product contamination of one shipment of Coca Cola in Belgium and Holland immediately affected Coca Cola sales across Europe. Macdonald's fought a court action with two unemployed

Londoners to refute their claims about its beef-sourcing policies. Despite its overwhelming resource advantage over its two opponents, and despite winning the court judgement, Macdonald's lost the enormous public relations battle that raged over the Internet throughout the case.

The rejection of genetically modified foods in Great Britain during 1999 was a popular information campaign that succeeded against strong opposition from corporate giants like Monsanto and the British Government. The entire British supermarket sector followed its customers into the anti-genetic modification lobby. Iceland, the freezer food chain, gained considerable first mover advantage by its immediate and heavily advertised decision not to stock GM foods.

Conclusion – the management challenge of knowledge application

This chapter started with a description of Tesco's Club Card as an example of knowledge management. It has not delivered Tesco into a 'Promised Land' of competitive invulnerability, but it has helped Tesco overtake Sainsbury's at the top of the retail tree and has pushed the whole of the British retail sector to improve its collection and use of customer information.

The pressure to manage knowledge better is no more and no less than a reflection of an increasingly competitive business environment. Tesco and its competitors are not just managing knowledge because they can, but because they have to. The possibilities knowledge management offers are made necessities by the forces of competition.

Having found out that they can improve business performance through managing knowledge, corporations now find that they must do it in order to keep hold of a market which is better able to act on information than ever before. But what should be the focus of knowledge management?

5

What knowledge needs managing?

Introduction

Corporations survive and prosper by focusing on their key value streams. They are the processes which most positively differentiate them from their competition. They are the differences on which managers build strategic positions, because they are not easily copiable.

There is a wonderful visual joke in Woody Allen's sci-fi comedy film *Sleeper* from the early 1970's. After a thousand years of sleep, he awakens and sets out to escape from the totalitarian state that rules Earth. In a cave full of twentieth century artefacts, he finds a Volkswagen Beetle. He jumps in and starts it with one turn of the key and drives off without comment. The gag was an ironic but implicitly positive expression of the popular view of Volkswagen's main product and core strength as a car-maker.

How did Volkswagen go about defending and building on such positive market perceptions of the Beetle? A real shop floor focus would have involved a continued concentration on it as a product. After all, the Beetle had carried Volkswagen to its high market rating. Yet managers at VW took the decision to let go of it[1]. Rather than hold tight to the symbol of their automotive engineering knowledge, VW let the Beetle market run down while

---

[1] A new version was reintroduced by Volkswagen more than a decade later.

it threw its corporate weight behind newer and wholly different models like the Golf and Polo. Managers took the view that the Beetle was not VW's strength, but just an expression of it – a reflection of its corporate knowledge capabilities.

Another interesting example is supplied by Apple. Apple was becoming more and more of a specialist niche supplier, more or less counted out of the wider personal computer market, after Microsoft established Windows and DOS as the industry-dominant operating system. Several high profile product launches from Apple failed to excite the market. Steve Jobs was discarded by Apple's board, and its outlook was gloomy.

Apple only recovered when Jobs returned and refocused the corporation on its market rather than its lead in design capabilities. The fastest selling personal computer of 1999 was not fundamentally better than the competition in any technical sense. It was differently coloured and differently shaped.

Apple's recovery and Volkswagen's long term strength are reflections of managerial concentration on the sources of the value their output generates, not just on the output itself. Volkswagen anticipated the fall from favour of its core product and engineered its way to a new position by launching new models before its market position was threatened. Steve Jobs turned Apple around before market goodwill and the most creative contributors at Apple had been lost, by returning to what had set it apart in the first place, a willingness to challenge conventional wisdom.

Managers who are content to monitor and manage the real shop floor without regard for the virtual would find it difficult to emulate them. How would they know where or when to start?

Knowledge worth knowing

Managers cannot just decide to share all knowledge or simply trust that worthwhile knowledge will emerge if they demand that their people seek it. Knowledge management can, however, focus on areas of knowledge that link to business objectives.

This is not as straightforward as it may seem. At lower levels, middle managers must look to the targets that are set for themselves, their teams and departments to define their business objectives. That means that senior managers must set business objectives that reflect a real appreciation of the nature and value of knowledge.

The focus of knowledge management

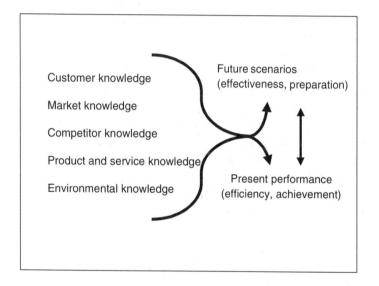

The diagram above illustrates the different elements in the focus of corporate knowledge management. Knowledge serves two primary functions within organisations. First, knowledge is what enables organisations to cope with an uncertain future. This involves recognising trends and opportunities, predicting coming events and, in general, making sense of the unfamiliar. Organisations are better able to cope when managers can picture possible future scenarios, either to make desired ones come about or to prepare the organisation for when a situation arises.

American information age philosopher Alvin Tofler coined the term *'future shock... the shattering stress and disorientation... induce*[d] *in individuals by... too much change in too short a time.'* John Blackwell at IBM actually lists *'fewer surprises'* amongst the benefits of knowledge management. A large proportion of management education and training has focused on the problem of motivating workforces. One of the most important elements in motivation is that people can see the sense in what they and their organisations are doing. Thus, one of the key effects of knowledge management is to motivate organisation members by helping ensure that the organisation is not too surprised by the unexpected future.

The second function of knowledge is to enable the efficient operation of the real shop floor. The development and sharing of practices and processes has been a primary aim of management throughout the twentieth century. Usually this means making tacit knowledge explicit and combining explicit knowledge. Benchmarking is an example of this knowledge management application.

The two functions are entirely complementary, because effective corporations attract no customers if they are not competitively efficient, while corporations attract no customers if they do not serve their markets efficiently. In hunting, for example, someone who is efficient in the operational process of shooting a gun must also be effective in the environmental process of stalking and finding game. Otherwise there is no food for the pot. Conversely, terrible shots will go hungry, however good they are at finding game.

Efficient real shop floors

Processes are learned and improved in most organisations due to widely shared and commonly understood notions of organisational purpose and environment. For instance, a sales team will usually have a team-wide appreciation of what its targets are, who are its main competitors and how buoyant the overall market is. Records will routinely be kept that show calls made, sales outcomes and contact names.

A whole range of useful conclusions can be drawn from taking such information and combining it with other information. For instance, area sales trends may reveal patterns that inform longer term advertising and production decisions. BT uses the timing of telephone line failures during electrical storms to understand and predict the effects of such storms as they advance. This can enable more efficient planning of emergency repairs, and so limit the overall impact of lightning strikes on the telephone system.

In general, real shop floor systems need to be designed to achieve efficient operation by reflecting what is known about the processes. Assembly lines are externalised representations of the expertise of designers, engineers and skilled craft workers. The philosophy behind Business Process Re-engineering is that the tacit knowledge of people about their own business processes can be made explicit and designed into the re-engineered process.

The trouble-shooter

In an influential British television series, Sir John Harvey-Jones, former chief executive of ICI, visited small businesses to advise them as a strategic consultant. There is one episode, much loved by lecturers and inflicted on under-graduate business studies students, in which he absolutely slates the owner-managers of Morgan Cars for their archaic craft-based and even chaotic approach to production and marketing. What becomes clear during the programme is that he and Morgan's management had entirely different notions of what they were trying to do.

They took a perverse pride in the six year customer waiting list and invited prospective owners down to the Morgan Works in South Wales to watch their luxury sports cars being crafted. Sir John saw a desperate need for a capital injection and a more systematic production process to lower waiting time. The entire debate was about real shop floor efficiency, but the actual disagreement was much more fundamental, it was about which type of market Morgan was in. Sir John was concerned to address the efficiency of a small car producer, but he would have done better to ask if Morgan was in the car market at all. What essential knowledge of the production and supply of luxuries to extremely wealthy (and patient!) customers might Morgan lose in the process of becoming a more cost efficient competitor along the lines of more mainstream automobile manufacturers?

There are many problems in making such knowledge explicit in the service of efficiency. One of the most persistent is that managers fail to understand that efficiency is an operational concept that depends for its definition on organisational objectives. Efficiency is an absolute target, while the causes that efficiency serves are ever moving. An assembly line or any similar explicit application of knowledge can become highly irrelevant when market conditions change. Late in 1999, British Gas announced the closure of a north London call centre made redundant by new technology less than five years after it had opened.

In 2000, BT has become a champion of mass customisation, that is, the customised combination of generic components to meet the individual needs of corporate customers. Similarly, domestic telephone customers choose from a menu of standard offerings to generate a specific service to meet their requirements. In the past, one undifferentiated service was available to all domestic customers and the primary challenge was to raise efficiency of supply. Today, improvements in information and communications technology have created such a fierce and changing competitive environment that it is far more important to focus on predicting and matching the shifting expectations of customers and the capabilities of competitors.

Effective organisations

The most efficient organisation in the world will fail if its capacities are applied to tasks that do not reflect its environmental needs. We use the term *fish out of water* to describe efficient people who are in a situation where their skills and abilities are not particularly useful.

> ### Bill and Ted's bogus adventure
>
> In the second of the 1980's Bill and Ted movies, the two moronic Californian teens are about to be taken by the Grim Reaper, when they challenge him to a contest for their lives. As the ultimate winner over all living things, the Reaper confidently agrees. Bill and Ted, though, have no trouble defeating Death at *battleships*, the time-killing study hall game played by high schoolers almost everywhere. The joke is that, for all the Grim Reaper's power, he is a fish out of water when faced with the empty-headed challenge from Bill and Ted.

For organisations to perform effectively, they must act in a way that is consistent with their environment. Sometimes this is entirely impossible. Britain's corner shops and their American Ma and Pa counterparts did not have the resources to respond effectively to the post-1945 rise of the supermarket and out-of-town shopping, no matter how clearly they foresaw it. The giants of the typewriting industry, Remington and Olivetti, ultimately proved just as unable to defend their office equipment market against the rise of information technology. They had the resources but lacked the corporate imagination.

Clayton Christiansen's excellent book *The Innovator's Dilemma* is subtitled *When New Technologies Cause Great Firms to Fail*. His argument is that the very thought processes, performance standards and beliefs that make great firms so great, also serve as barriers when it comes to recognising the competitive threat posed by new technologies.

From a knowledge management perspective, corporations achieve greatness through their capacity to make the real shop floor efficiently accomplish tasks which make the corporation effective within its environment. According to Christiansen, their success contributes to a kind of organisational inertia that makes it almost impossible for the organisation to respond adequately when new technologies alter their environment. Their present market dominance blinds them to the possibility of a future in which different technologies could make them ineffective.

The evidence gathered by Christiansen in support of his hypothesis is impressive. Two examples will suffice:

- Control Data, the market leader in the 14 inch disc drive market in the 1970's, only introduced an 8 inch version for the minicomputer market three years after the market emerged and never captured as much as 1% of the new market.
- Discount retailing in America moved from holding under 10% of department store, drug and variety store sales in 1959 to nearly 40% in 1966, but only Kresge (with K-Mart) and Dayton-Hudson (with Target) succeeded in migrating with the market. Not one of the other traditional retailers was able to establish a significant discount retailing presence. Sears Roebuck, the most admired and dominant retailer of that era, very nearly went under and is now just another player in a crowded market. F.W. Woolworth (no relation to the British high street retailer with the same name) was, in 1959, one of the leading variety store chains. Its effort to match Kresge with Woolco utterly failed. In 1998, F.W. Woolworth decided to close its last stores.

The previous chapter showed how the business environment is changing at an accelerating rate in response to a range of different forces:

- The world is a simpler place to do business in than it used to be.
- Lean and fit organisations may do things better, but they are not necessarily better at changing what they do.
- Knowledge workers are powerful and valuable people who are reviewing their roles as employees.
- Customers manage knowledge.

As the figure below shows, firms are being pressed by markets to do things quicker, better and cheaper. These forces have contributed to a need both for increasing efficiency in activities and increasing flexibility to stay effective. There is more to do, but less time to do it in and to reap the benefits when things are done well.

Trends in the business environment

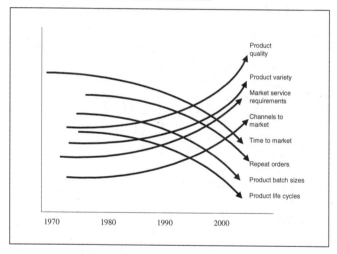

Types of knowledge

For most organisations the principal sorts of knowledge worth knowing can be grouped under four headings:

- Customer knowledge
- Market knowledge
- Product and service knowledge
- Environmental knowledge.

Customer knowledge

This is specific knowledge of the existing customer base. There is an essential minimum level of customer knowledge without which no corporation can survive long. Corporations need to know what customers buy, how much they buy, and technical, financial and related issues arising from supplying them.

Such knowledge is essential to commerce. Its absence makes supply nearly impossible. Companies that do not keep such basic records are unable to do the most basic administrative jobs and are unlikely to last long.

Usually, explicitly kept customer knowledge is limited to the sort of material that enables administration and fits comfortably in standard information management systems. It gives little flavour of what is actually involved in satisfying demand. For real appreciation of the individual characteristics of customers, one must usually look to the tacit knowledge possessed by individual sales people about their clients.

Sometimes this is vital. Early in her sales career a friend, a successful sales manager, used her company's normal logistics supplier to send a major export order to Germany, unaware that the customer had its own shipping arrangements. The customer was neither amused nor understanding and her employer had to pay the shipping costs itself. The previous holder of her post had either forgotten, or had chosen not to pass on, his tacit knowledge. Her managers were unaware of the issue at all until the customer's complaint arrived. The information could have and should have been explicitly available to her.

Beyond such knowledge of what the customer purchases and how they prefer to be supplied, there is also the knowledge that the customer possesses about how they use what they purchase and what their future plans are. Accessing such customer knowledge can enable suppliers to improve their service to match their customers' changing needs more precisely. Corporations such as Hewlett-Packard have developed their communications networks so that suppliers and customers can have appropriate extranet access.

Market knowledge

This is what is known about the wider market from which actual customers emerge. We have already seen that information about the business environment is becoming more readily available and accessible. That makes it increasingly important that organisations know about their markets, and are aware of what they know.

Professor Michael Thomas of the University of Strathclyde highlights the ways in which the market environment has changed in the information and communications technology era, and argues that the changes make markets much more knowable and exploitable[2]. He both welcomes *'the death of distance'* as an opportunity to market more effectively and warns, that the increasing accessibility of market information will create a hierarchy in which knowledge of the basis of the environment is more important than other knowledge because:

'This is emphatically not the global village, rather it is... a society structured around networks... This network architecture is dynamic, open ended, flexible and able to extend endlessly by passing/disconnecting undesirable components.'

Those on top will be the ones who understand their relationship with the network, because they are best placed to understand their successes and failures, and so cope with the continuous changeability of markets. Their position is derived from the capacities of their knowledge work. They can strengthen network connections that less knowledgeable competitors neither understand nor control.

Some of the fastest growing corporations appear to move almost effortlessly into markets on the strength of their tacit knowledge, what Thomas Stewart[3] calls *'an unexpressed and possibly inexpressible "feel" for the market.'* Yet, they can be the most vulnerable, because they lack insight into how and why they succeed. A classic

---

[2] M. J. Thomas, 'The information age and the death of distance', ICCM, UMIST, July 1999.

[3] Thomas Stewart, *Intellectual Capital*, Nicholas Brealey, London, 1997.

example was supplied by Sir Clive Sinclair. Largely self-taught, Sir Clive founded Sinclair Research in 1979, and launched the phenomenally successful ZX 80 computer, which was sold at the rate of 10,000 a month. Its replacements, the ZX 81and ZX Spectrum were equally popular. At its peak in 1983, the Spectrum sold at a rate of 12,000 per month.

Sir Clive's phenomenal tacit knowledge of the home computer market was transferred to the electric car market, when he launched the infamous Sinclair C5 three wheeler. Investors scrambled for a share of his Midas touch. The C5 proved an absolute disaster and virtually broke the firm. In retrospect, it seems incredible that so much effort and money were invested in the C5, but the success of the ZX computers had created a blind faith in Sir Clive's tacit market knowledge. It was misplaced.

Product and service knowledge

This kind of knowledge is gathered as a matter of course, but its use is rarely well-managed. Examples that I have seen include the following:

- The chemical information system supplier that set up three teams to remove what turned out to be the same programme bug reported by different customers in different market regions.
- The newly floated global networking corporation which published contradictory prices and specifications on its German, English and French language pages, a blunder that a competitor was pleased to share with the trade press.
- The English local authority committee which disbanded and dispersed its successful Y2K project team at the same time as another committee was setting up a team to manage the conversion of IT systems to handle the new common European currency.

What is most usually meant when corporations are redefined as knowledge-based is that they will refocus on design and service to meet customer demands rather than merely using design and service to support production. Thus IBM is no longer a supplier of computer hardware so much as a supplier of total corporate solutions that may involve computer hardware (and may not). In the words of IBM Chairman and CE, Lou Gerstner, in IBM's 1998 Annual Report:

> *'However, technology changes much too quickly now for any company to build a sustainable competitive advantage on that basis alone. Someone is always inventing some software code or device that is a little faster or cheaper. More and more, the winning edge comes from how you help customers use technology to steal a march on their competitors, to implement entirely new business models. That means creating integrated solutions that draw on the full range of solutions and, increasingly, services. And it means connecting the dots between what you learn in the lab and what you learn in the marketplace.'*

People often dismiss such statements as mere words. An automobile executive once criticised a similar statement from Ford on the grounds that their core business would remain building cars. But, he was missing the point. At the heart of the typical automobile maker's purpose is the manufacture and sale of cars. Design, service and finance are necessary support services. They may be profitable, but the core function, manufacture and supply, is the key and will get the lion's share of management attention. The knowledge-based automobile supplier's purpose, on the other hand, is to help customers gain the best use from cars. Design and service provision are core functions. Manufacture is an important element in the process, but no more so than are the others. Take service provision; the evidence is that customers are more likely to stay loyal to a less reliable car if it is supported by high-quality service than they are to a more reliable car with poor service support.

Environmental knowledge

One of the most influential and, certainly, the best-selling guru books of the 1980's was Peters and Waterman's *In Search of*

Excellence[4]. Its essential message was a simple one: the best managed companies were those in which senior managers communicated with their workforces. Peters and Waterman coined the term MBWA, management by walking about, to describe how managers could find out what their people knew about the business environment. In most of their examples, MBWA was no metaphor, the excellent managers apparently did walk about. There may have been some morale-raising benefits arising from their hikes, and they certainly inspired loyalty and greater effort in many employees, but it is doubtful that managers gained much knowledge about their global corporations from the views of a small number of geographically concentrated employees[5].

More than that, as organisational development consultant Roger Harrison[6] observed, such *excellent* companies may lose track of the environment as they become consumed by their own visions:

> *'Such an organisation may over-rely upon its vision to organise the work and may have inadequate and under-utilised systems. It may develop an elitist faith in its own dream and become unresponsive to disconfirming information from the wider environment.'*

Any reasonably complex or large organisation interacts with its external environment in an enormous number of ways. The flow of environmental knowledge into it is, thus, a rich and varied source of signals helping it ensure it is positioned to be effective and able to stay efficient. The challenge is to consistently find ways to recognise, harvest and learn from the environmental knowledge that flows into the organisation over time. Harrison's warnings are supported by the rapid fall from their *excellent* positions of so many of Peters and Waterman's examples. They could not keep it up.

Most managers are familiar with terms like environmental scanning, PEST (political-economic-social-technological) or SWOT

---

[4] Peters and Waterman, *In Search of Excellence*, Harper & Row, New York, 1992.

[5] What would the average worker in your organisation say if the Chief Executive appeared at their elbow?

[6] Roger Harrison, *A Consultant's Journey*, Jossey-Bass, San Francisco, 1995.

(strengths-weaknesses-opportunities-threats) analysis. They are the bread-and-butter concepts of business study courses. Their presence does not, unfortunately, constitute environmental knowledge management because they are usually associated with the annual preparation of business plans and are most often the responsibility of specialised and senior 'strategic' managers. Effective environmental knowledge management requires that the organisation is able to receive new knowledge and to use it. Knowledge must not be disregarded just because it comes from the 'wrong' sources or if it conflicts with dominant thinking.

Two children's stories

Most of us know the story of *The Emperor's New Clothes*. It tells how the Emperor and all his empire join in praising the sheerness and lightness of his wonderful new clothes, when in fact he is naked. No one can see his nudity because emperors do not go around naked. A naked emperor makes no sense, until one young ne'er-do-well points out the obvious. The story ends with the previously worshipful subjects roaring with laughter at the Emperor's humiliation as he stumbles off to get dressed.

When my daughters were young I recall another story[7] of a little boy who wanders into a palace where he finds and puts on the official robes of the Royal Adviser. In these robes, he is rushed to the King and questioned on matters of state. Meanwhile, the real Royal Adviser, lacking his robes, is thrown into the dungeon, unrecognised, for presuming to advise the King. The little boy's inability to answer leads to more aggressive questioning and the little boy starts to cry. The questioning turns to ridicule. As he howls louder, the King scornfully shouts, 'ROYAL ADVISERS DON'T CRY! LITTLE BOYS CRY! YOU'RE JUST A little boy…' At last they see the child inside the official robes.

---

[7] Though not, alas, the author or title, so there is no reference, for which I apologise.

Two knowledge management questions for each story:

1. In the first story, was the Emperor naked before the boy shouted out?
2. Would it matter if the Emperor was naked or not, if the boy had kept quiet about his observation?
3. In the second story, was the quality of the Royal Adviser's advice determined by its content or by the robes of office?
4. How should kings tell royal advisers from little boys?

One of the best histories in the development of management concerns W. Edwards Deming whose notion that the market would prefer Total Quality was rejected by American managers as more expensive than budgeting for acceptable levels of error. Then his message was taken on board in Japan and returned to haunt American businesses in the form of market share and profits lost to Japanese competitors. The initial American and European response was to explain the undeniable environmental change as due to inherently Japanese qualities that could not be duplicated elsewhere. It took many years for American and European managers to revise their notions in a way that made it possible to see Japanese businesses as enough like Western ones to justify trying to understand what they were doing. Deming took pleasure in pointing out that his principles of Total Quality Management were developed in the United States, before he ever went to Japan.

Conclusion – the managerial challenge of recognising the virtual shop floor

Observe how your organisation operates and you will usually find an overwhelming managerial preoccupation with the real shop floor. The pressure is on to do better than the competition. Your most recent brush with consultants was in search of dramatically improved productivity and competitiveness. Costs have got to come down, because prices surely will.

For most managers, that is a fair description of their working environment. At the more senior level, you are setting and enforcing the targets under the critical eye of your boards and shareholders. The middle and junior managers are, in turn, striving to achieve the targets set by senior management. Managers are judged, ultimately, by what happens on the real shop floor. The common denominator for the different types of knowledge is their organisational purpose. Organisations need to be efficient and they need to be effective. The knowledge processes of the virtual shop floor make it possible to design effective real shop floor activities and to undertake them efficiently.

One way or another, managers will seek to make their organisations efficient and effective, and they will do so by drawing on the knowledge they possess. Those managers who understand this will recognise that it requires them to manage knowledge explicitly. To trust that unmanaged, hidden and haphazard knowledge flows will prove adequate is not a safe option.

6

The processes of knowledge management

'Knowledge in an organisation is widely dispersed and assumes many forms, but its quality is revealed in the range of capabilities that it possesses as a result of this knowledge. While most of the organisation's knowledge is rooted in the expertise and experience of its individual members, the organisation provides a physical, social and cultural context so that the exercise and growth of this knowledge takes on meaning and purpose.'

CHUN WEI CHOO[1]

Introduction

The processes of knowledge management are many and varied. Managers cannot simply copy the practices of others, because each organisation faces a different set of knowledge management problems. Why this is so is explained in this chapter. The chapter

---

[1] His book, *The Knowing Organization*, from which this quote is taken, is by far the best high level academic text I have found on this subject.

explores the role of organisational context in defining the knowledge management challenge.

No knowledge management tool will work if it is not applied in a manner that is sensitive to the way its users think and behave. In every organisation knowledge processes are primarily tacit and hidden on the virtual shop floor. Approaches described in this chapter have achieved spectacular successes, and failures. Which result depends on how well managers understand their purposes and the processes of their own virtual shop floors.

A health warning – there is no best practice

People do not enter management to spend their time theorising about the meanings and concepts behind business. They do it to change and develop things through management. Ideas are tools for achieving ends and debates are means of better understanding tools, so they can be better utilised. I have lost track of the number of conferences I have attended where speakers are judged and dismissed as *'too academic'*.

If you have managed to get this far in the book, though, you will know that knowledge management requires managers to hold off using the tools and to reflect on the meanings and concepts that exist within their organisations first. It is not just a case of finding and copying someone else's successful initiative. As John Seely Brown, Director of Xerox PARC, argues, *'Trying to convert tacit knowledge to explicit knowledge and move it is trying to convert "knowing" to information... it doesn't work.'*

This is profoundly gloomy news for corporations that have got by in the past by defensively copying *'first in the field'* leaders, a tried and trusted approach that can work well when corporations follow the product leaders fast enough. It does not work, though, when knowledge is involved, because knowledge processes are everywhere unique and uncopiable. It is no surprise that the longstanding champions of second-in-the-market strategies such as Britain's Marks & Spencer and Sainsbury's have found themselves less able to cope when competitors like Next, River Island, Tesco and ASDA have developed flexible strategies built on knowledge processes. To match effective knowledge managers, corporations have to understand and align their own knowledge systems.

There are standard knowledge management tools and processes, but how they are developed and used will be different in each organisation. Thus, knowledge management solutions cannot be taken off the shelf and applied freely. In chapter three, I introduced the *second principle* of knowledge management: Knowledge management is primarily the management of the processes that generate knowledge, rather than the management of knowledge itself. It is the key to understanding why knowledge management implementations succeed or fail. There is no single best practice.

No manager should seek to apply a knowledge management solution without reading John Seely Brown's health warning:

'*Knowledge management has made no progress towards understanding why* [managing knowledge is] ... *so hard because knowledge management makes no clear distinction between knowledge and information. Information is fundamentally dis-embedable and therefore transportable and re-embedable. Knowledge is not. If you try to move best practices as information, and expect people to absorb them, you're guaranteed to fail. End of story.*'

Finding knowledge – seeing through a different lens

One of the most immediate challenges facing those interested in knowledge management is how to stop the haemorrhaging of knowledge that accompanies the failure to manage it. Paul Pederson of PriceWaterhouseCoopers points out that about two-thirds of employees made redundant in 1994 in the United States were educated to university level and speculates about the possible value of the knowledge lost with them[2].

---

[2] Paul Pederson, 'Q&A', *Knowledge Management Review*, no. 5, November–December 1998.

In the same article, he describes an anonymous insurance company that slimmed down its claims department to speed up and lower the cost of processing major claims only to find that the people who left were those who were the most experienced claims evaluators. New losses through overly-generous settlements easily offset the cost and speed gains. I was recently asked to instruct on a post-graduate degree for a British university where the development of a new course had gone ahead alongside the unremarked departure of several of the specialist academic staff needed to deliver it[3].

Choo's description of knowledge in organisations at the start of this chapter helps capture the quandary of tool choice nicely. Knowledge and the capacity to learn mainly reside in individuals, but the physical, social and cultural context provided by the organisation is what gives value to knowledge.

Knowledge in context

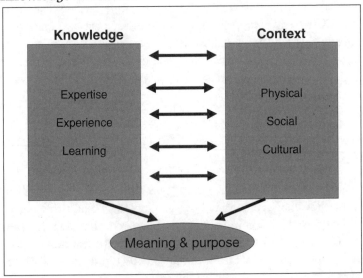

---

[3] You guessed. It was a course in knowledge management! Without wishing to make exaggerated claims for my own Sheffield Business School, I must point out that the university in question is located elsewhere.

Many initiatives disappoint because of the failure to acknowledge this contextual relationship. Our two principles of knowledge management point towards the need to ground systems in contexts meaningful to users. Managers who look to purchase knowledge management tools, and consultants who offer them, need to remember that the same tools can prove enormously successful or abject failures in different situations and in different organisations. Those that have failed have generally been the ones applied without adequate appreciation of the significance of the context, as illustrated above.

This applies to every significant development. An example is set out in the matrix below. The company wanted to set up an intranet and used a simple matrix to place the project in context. The project team identified a need to focus on the new intranet as a system to help people share. The traditional systems dichotomy between developers and users (sharers) was down-played, and it was proposed that the intranet be presented to employees as a means of stabilising the company after a period of unsettling change.

The intranet implementation project

Objectives	Starting position	Ideal approach
Ensuring sensible design of content pages	• General inexperience in design concepts outside IT department • General inexperience in intranet use	• Management sets parameters and facilitates design process • Management/sharers enforce compliance
Ensuring content meets user needs	• User needs unknown • Users accustomed to other media	• Sharers negotiate content in their joint roles as users/providers • Sharers use what they need, discarding the rest
Ensuring extensive and growing use of the intranet	• Significant downsizing in progress • Two recent mergers • Many job re-definitions and transfers • Insecurity common	• Sharers feel unthreatened • Sharers gain benefits • Sharers trust the system

This matrix was used to frame the project. The project team was aware that the ideal approach was unachievable, but they were able to use the framework to agree realistic movement from the unacceptable initial position.

Sometimes there is no gradual way to move from an unacceptable current position. At Hewlett-Packard it was recognised that its dominance of the laser printer market was an insurmountable obstacle to a change towards the emerging ink-jet technology. H-P's solution was to set up a wholly separate H-P company to develop the market for ink-jet printers.

Almost certainly, if the ink-jet effort had been undertaken within the existing H-P corporate structure, H-P would not have achieved its dominant market position in the supply of ink-jet printers. H-P was the established leader in laser jet technology, which was popular with customers. The new company, though, was not held back by its commitment to the dominant technology and customer base. Its research and development efforts were not split between the two technologies. Its sales force was not dividing its attention between the familiar and high value (and high commission!) laser printers and the unfamiliar, technically inferior and lower value (and low commission!) ink-jets.

Recognising the strategic purpose of knowledge

The meaning and purpose of knowledge depends on its strategic purpose. Michael Zack of Boston's Northeastern University has explored the strategic issues raised by knowledge management for a number of years. He characterises knowledge by focusing on its opposite, ignorance. According to him, ignorance arises from four sources:

- Uncertainty – lack of enough information
- Complexity – having too much information to process into an understandable and useful form
- Ambiguity – lacking a framework for interpreting information
- Equivocality – having more than one competing frame, and so multiple and conflicting meanings.

Uncertainty

Uncertainty is an information problem. It can arise because key people have been let go or because of poor internal communication. The departure of middle managers during the series of downsizing and re-engineering exercises of the past fifteen years, for example, left many organisations ignorant of how they had developed and implemented systems and contracts which required renewal.

A prime example is supplied by the network of automated transaction machines and the Y2K problem. The banks discovered the need for Cobol programmers to make their ATM network Y2K compliant after they had dispensed with their Cobol programmers. Equally, the emergence of a new technology may leave established users of the old technology struggling to find information about it and unable to plan a strategy until they do.

As often as the organisation lacks the knowledge, it possesses knowledge but is unable to share it with the people who could use it. Typically in many organisations help desk queries are logged individually so that there is often an enormous amount of duplicated problem-solving when similar queries go unmatched. One of the prime aims of information systems is to supply a technically efficient means of overcoming this form of uncertainty.

The reason why such uncertainty is more than an information management problem lies on the right hand side of the Knowledge in Context illustration on p. 108. Technically efficient systems may not be used efficiently because people do not understand or trust them as much as they trust more traditional methods of communicating or because people are unwilling to share what they know. When people feel insecure, knowledge is power and goes unshared.

Complexity

Complexity is another form of information problem. It is more usually characterised as information overload. There is so much data that could be relevant that it clogs the system. The first knowledge management principle states: The value of information is determined by its recipients and not by its senders. If we don't receive it, understand it, don't believe it or cannot see a use for it, it is worthless data. When an environment grows too complex, information loses value. Key points get overlooked. Every executive who is forced by the sheer volume of e-mail to put in extra hours of work will recognise the dangers of complexity. The great advantage of the Internet, its comprehensiveness, is also its weakness. We can go straight from situations of uninformed uncertainty to over-informed complexity with one hit of the search button.

E-mail solutions involve improved information filters, tighter control of e-mail protocols and rights to cut down on the volume that people receive. More general information solutions involve improved database indexing and search tools. The general aim is to ensure that only the most *relevant* information reaches people and they are shielded from complexity. The problem with filters in particular, though, is that decisions about the value of information are made without the potential recipient ever seeing it. There is a risk that genuinely effective filters can confine people's thinking 'in boxes'.

One of the most frequently seen signals of complexity is that people opt out of systems such as intranets. They prefer old low tech communications that are familiar and do not overload them. A common management mistake is to define the problem as technical and replace the system with one that can handle more information faster, a response which merely increases the information overload.

Ambiguity

Ambiguity is more difficult, because it arises when an organisation cannot interpret information. More information will not help if its meaning goes unrecognised. Chris Argyris calls this phenomenon *'doom-loop learning'*. Information is rejected or ignored, because it does not fit with the mass of information that is expected or desired.

Organisations in ambiguous situations keep on doing what they have always done. Like overconfident drivers in a strange country they pass signs that mean nothing to them, because they lack a frame of reference. For all that the drivers can tell, the sign might be advertising the desired destination or warning that a bridge has collapsed.

A colleague at a trade fair in China once watched a competitor, new in the market, with a highly sought-after product to sell. In the space of an hour he watched the competitor turn four hot leads into 'no sales' by shovelling eagerly proffered business cards straight into his pocket. He did not know that he had entered an environment where the handling of business cards sent different social messages.

Closed minds and closed mines

Early in the 1980's, I started working in an economic research section for Barnsley Council, a local authority in Yorkshire that had been utterly dependent on coal mining for its economic and social well-being for more than 150 years. Nearly one in five of its workforce depended directly on the coal industry for employment.

As the research section began collecting more and more information about the imminent collapse of mining, there was little response from the political leadership of the council. There had always been crises in mining, which eventually ended in compromises between the nationalised corporation, British Coal, and the union, the National Union of Mineworkers. Continuous bickering between the union and management had gone on as long as anyone could remember.

Council leaders could not imagine that their main industry was under a different and more severe threat after so many false alarms. They continued to believe in their hearts that the National Union of Mineworkers and British Coal would sort out their differences as they always had. One or two local mines might shut, but most of the miners would be transferred to another local colliery. They held to their beliefs long after it was clear to outside observers that the real problem was that globalisation had opened up Great Britain's coal market to other coal suppliers and competion from other fuels like gas. Within ten years, all sixteen local coal mines and 20,000 jobs had gone.

Ambiguous situations require reframed questions, but these are particularly hard to ask, because they require genuinely creative thinking. Much of the difficulty managers have in understanding knowledge management is because it is an ambiguous concept. The most commonly aired practical criticism of knowledge management is that it allows no clear business metrics to tell us how much it contributes to the bottom line. To gain such a measure would require knowledge processes to be somehow isolated as a separate function from other functions, an impossible notion, because knowledge creation and sharing are what inform and enable the whole process of supplying customers. What is required is a reframing of the question to remove its ambiguity.

Learning to count what really counts

'Measurement has a strong impact on behaviour. People know that under or outperforming the measures bring punishment or reward and act accordingly. Hence, the management cliché that what's measured gets managed. "You get what you count," says consultant John Seddon of Vanguard Consulting.

'But few managers realise that that is precisely what makes management such a two-edged weapon. Wrong measures equals wrong behaviour. Moreover, not everything should be measured anyway. As Einstein put it, "Not everything that counts can be counted. And not everything that can be counted, counts."

'Quality guru W. Edwards Deming, a hard-headed statistician, believed that 97% of what mattered in a business couldn't be measured – qualities such as intelligence, integrity, imagination, genuine customer friendliness. Unfortunately, the unquantifiable is harder to manage than budgets, targets and standards – so managers spend almost all their time managing the numbers.'

Simon Caulkin, *The Observer*, 16 May 1999

Equivocality

The last of the four forms of organisational ignorance is equivocality. The information is available, but people are attaching different and incompatible meanings to it. Half empty cups are also half full. Opportunities can be threats. Equivocality is always present because no two people can ever see the world the same way, but it is also always increased by poor communication and inadequate collaboration.

Organisations that equivocate develop conflicting strategies or inconsistent operations that leave customers confused and dissatisfied. They lack unity of purpose and lack confidence in direction. This form of ignorance is most commonly seen in organisations that have dominated markets but come under threat from disruptive new competitors.

The people and divisions in the front line see what is happening, but they struggle to make others, protected by distance, organisational inertia and reserves of fat, understand. When Ford introduced its compact sporty Mustang in the 1960's, it was so different from Ford's traditional offerings that it was referred to as the *'unFord.'* Unfortunately, Mustang's success placed it firmly in the Ford mainstream, where it was managed like any other successful Ford offering. Ford did not set out to change the Mustang. It was just that in Detroit in the 1960's car models were *improved* annually through the addition of extras. In a few short years the *'unFord'* had put on more than a tonne in weight and a foot in length. It was no longer a sporty compact at all. The Japanese and Germans gratefully filled the market niche that Mustang had proven and then abandoned.

Hitting targets and losing customers

I recently encountered a conflict between a sales team and an accounts team. Both had just returned from motivational sessions with the MD and senior managers where they had been urged to work harder to make their procedures work and to hit targets. The sales people responded by gaining a £20,000 order from a longstanding but previously much smaller scale customer. The accounts team responded by putting a stop on the new order, because of a disputed return note for less than £100 that had been unresolved for more than six months and had been singled out by management as an example of the sloppy accounting practices that had to be tightened up. Both the sale and its halt were inspired by the same initiative. The customer withdrew the order and found a new supplier.

Equivocal ignorance does not just lead to internal strife. At Singer in the 1970's, the corporation followed an active recruitment policy to take advantage of the increasing shift of women from home-making back into the employment market. Yet, at the same time, it was pressurising its sales and marketing people over falling sewing machine sales. Singer had taken advantage of the labour market trend, but not recognised the implications for the sewing machine market. Women in work had less time to spend sewing and more income to buy clothes off the rack.

Ignorance is not bliss

Organisations that do not understand the nature of their ignorance will be likely to implement solutions that do not address the nature of their strategic knowledge problems. This is because the unrecognised ignorance is based on tacit assumptions that are unlikely to be recognised. The organisation will drift into deeper and deeper trouble because its strategies and activities unconsciously reinforce the ignorance.

The main lesson from organisational ignorance is that it causes troubles that appear as individual incidents or mistakes that can be corrected, without it ever being recognised that they are symptoms of a deeper failure to know what is going on. The individual mistakes may be corrected, but will be followed by more frequent and more serious incidents until the nature of the ignorance is perceived and acknowledged, or the organisation fails. Lou Gerstner's first achievement in turning around IBM in 1993 was persuading the organisation to understand just how deep a hole it was in.

Before any problem can be solved, it needs to be understood. As an inexperienced consultant I often complained about the unreasonableness of clients, but I am now convinced that the issue was usually equivocality or ambiguity at the project definition stage. Either I did not understand exactly what the client was expecting or different managers within the client organisation had conflicting expectations that could not all be satisfied.

It also needs to be understood that knowledge problems are intertwined. Ambiguity may be clarified only to give way to equivocality. Both could be happening against a backdrop of uncertainty or complexity. Much difficulty in the management of knowledge can be avoided by exploring the nature of corporate ignorance at the start of the project. Otherwise, individuals, teams and departments will separately develop their own solutions that will almost certainly conflict and lead to under-performance, social conflicts and even project failure.

Ignorance in practice

At Sheffield Business School, we are dealing with a strategic knowledge problem even as I write. We run a set of specialist Masters degrees and propose to integrate the teaching, administration and project development systems into a single knowledge management system. One of our earliest challenges was to identify an appropriate IT platform to support it. Our problem was that we did not understand well enough the competing merits of different systems.

We opted for a Lotus Domino environment, but did not understand the difference between using the Domino platform to develop our own templates or using Lotus' dedicated Domino education template, LearningSpace. Our Lotus contacts, in turn, may have been too ready to assume that we were entirely clear on the exact nature of the decision and that, as an educational institution, we would naturally want LearningSpace.

It took seven months of internal and external discussions and investigation to clarify our ambiguous understanding of the platforms. We reached a stage where different managers had to reconcile their differing equivocal positions that reflected the way that they individually overcame their initial ignorance. It was a slow process forced on us by our failure to address our ignorance at the very start as a team. Individual members committed to conflicting problem definitions and solutions, even though we met regularly and often commented on our uncertainty about the technology during meetings. Our initial failure contributed to a much more complex impasse involving personalities and wider organisational politics.

The learning process has been useful, but more thought at the start would have saved time and stress.

Knowledge management practices – building on environmental and strategic understanding

There are many tools that can enable and improve knowledge management in organisations. The Internet is full of homepages, so-called *'white papers'* and the like, which describe bespoke knowledge management solutions in considerable detail. The key to understanding their potential for good or ill lies in our first two tools, contextual framing and strategic purpose.

Procrustean logic

In Greek legend there was a giant pirate called Procrustes, who lured travellers into his house where he placed them on one of his special beds where they were held until ransomed by their friends. In order to encourage rapid turnover, Procrustes used the beds to reshape his hostages to fit them. Tall hostages were gradually shortened and short ones lengthened by various torturous means. Friends knew that they had to pay quickly if they wanted back a living hostage. Procrustes was himself treated to his own bed with fatal consequences by the hero Theseus, but not before he gave the world the term 'Procrustean logic', which means to shape reality to fit your view of it.

Knowledge management solutions are too often exercises in Procrustean logic. Universal tools that are applied in a manner that ignores the context and the nature of the strategic knowledge problem. Such solutions are almost inevitably doomed to fail. They clash too directly with overall direction and beliefs in the wider organisation to be accepted.

Sharing knowledge – two success stories

1. The experience of Buckman Laboratories illustrates how an information and communication network can serve as a knowledge management framework. Buckman Laboratories is a specialist in chemicals technology solutions. It has always traded on the knowledge of its workforce. Its problem was how to leverage what its associates knew more effectively, when they were based all over the world and were more often with clients or travelling than on Buckman sites. Chairman and CEO, Robert Buckman, has been personally driving the company's commitment to knowledge management for more than a decade. The key to Buckman's approach is knowledge sharing more than knowledge creation.

Their knowledge management solution is embedded in a system called '*K'Netix*'. It consists of a set of closed communities based on topics such as industrial technologies, markets, leisure and corporate developments. Buckman associates are encouraged to participate in the Buckman communities via K'Netix. Buckman's 12,000 associates are assessed in part by how they both contribute and draw from K'Netix. In 1997 Buckman told a World Trade Conference, '*We will no longer promote people who do not proactively share.*'

Buckman's K'Netix is built on the following principles:

- Eliminate gatekeepers so that everyone is responsible for their own knowledge and information is undistorted by intermediaries.
- Middle managers to act as mentors and project supporters rather than information controllers.
- Everyone at Buckman can access the system.
- Participation in K'Netix is a formal and appraised job requirement.

The costs of the system to Buckman average about £7,500 per employee annually, including all hardware, software and network charges, telephone charges, libraries and information systems. This works out as 3.5 to 4.5% of corporate revenue.

2. At Andersen Consulting, the challenge has been perceived as how to eliminate the twin problems of complexity and uncertainty across a decentralised global consultancy with 40,000 employees turning over $5 billion annually. Andersen's approach is built on a technically capable global information system, *'Knowledge Exchange,'* and a strictly defined notion of appropriate behaviour.

- Every project is entered in summary onto the global Andersen database with authors named.
- All reusable outputs (presentations and reports) are entered into the database and linked to summaries.
- Close attention to the categorisation of entries by industry and functional competencies.
- Prompt entry of material on database seen as essential to the role of all consultants.
- Requests for further information to be answered within 48 hours regardless of time pressures.

The Andersen Consulting approach seeks to manage explicit knowledge both to avoid reproducing it and to enable a trail to the possessors of tacit knowledge. As with Buckman Laboratories, it depends on powerful social pressures to make it effective. If, for example, consultants stopped entering explicit knowledge and responding to requests for tacit knowledge, the system would rapidly lose its usefulness. In part to reinforce and support participation, Andersen Consulting appoints regional and functional knowledge managers who are responsible for ensuring that their business units contribute in a manner consistent with the centrally designated concepts.

Both of these corporations have a number of advantages that have made it easier for them than it might be for others to manage knowledge. These include:

- Senior champions – as in practically every successful major corporate initiative, strong senior driving has been apparent at every stage.

- A large proportion of highly educated consultants in the workforce – they are accustomed to using electronic media to research and communicate.
- Highly dispersed and travelling workforces – there is little opportunity for an efficient, more sociable, informal network to compete with the knowledge management systems.
- Powerful shared visions and cultures – these are important factors in limiting perceptions of ambiguity or equivocal interpretations of information. Employees are confident that they share understanding and viewpoints without having to test each other.

Other corporations are making similar efforts. PriceWaterhouse-Coopers has made good knowledge management practices a prerequisite for promotion, while Chaparral Steel awards pay rises based on acquired and demonstrated skills.

Conclusion – being a knowledge manager

The starting point in any knowledge management initiative must be an understanding of its organisational context. The social acceptability of changing knowledge processes is the vital key to their success. Some organisations, like Buckman Laboratories or Andersen Consulting, may start with certain advantages, but all organisations have their individual contexts that require uniquely tailored solutions. Understanding the context of the knowledge management initiative is more important than any other single factor.

The second element in achieving a positive knowledge management solution lies in an understanding of the strategic nature of the knowledge problem.

Ignorance can arise from a range of causes. Lack of information is only one, and the least difficult to overcome. More difficult are the cases when ignorance is due to too much information or when it is interpreted equivocally or ambiguously. The practice of knowledge management depends on understanding the nature of the ignorance it seeks to combat.

7

Being a knowledge manager

Introduction

Our people are our most valuable asset!

In 1997, the European Foundation for Quality Management (EFQM) published the results of a European corporate survey which revealed *'that knowledge is second only to people in terms of an organisation's most prized assets.'*

Why, if not for their knowledge, and willingness to apply it, are people valued in European corporations?

What does it mean to be a knowledge manager or to manage knowledge while being a functional manager? Readers should know that they are already, and have always been, knowledge managers. Everyone participates as fully on the virtual shop floor as they do on the real one. Decisions to limit coffee breaks, close the smoking room or do anything else that affects communication, learning and doing are knowledge management decisions just as much as operational management ones. So, all of us are knowledge managers. In this chapter we explore some of the issues that arise in being *conscious* knowledge managers.

Main elements in knowledge management

There are three main elements in the management of knowledge:

- Purpose – there have to be objectives in mind for knowledge management to succeed. It may be a specific target such as a 10% improvement in sales or something more conceptual, like greater awareness of the relationship between financial management and the organisation's capacity to innovate.
- Means – we have already looked at general tools and processes, but how does one move beyond them to actually achieve knowledge management ends?
- Metrics – knowledge management defies traditional accountancy measures because of the way it cuts across traditional functional disciplines. How is a manager to know if knowledge management is having any effect at all?

Purpose

Knowledge management initiatives must start with an appreciation of purpose. Geoff Smith, the business development manager for Knowledge Transformation Services at Cap Gemini UK, warns against a lack of ambition in knowledge management, '... *in more and more cases, knowledge is the business, and... KM is not simply an advanced form of librarianship.*' He is concerned that knowledge management should not become an extension of information management.

The diagram opposite offers a simple grid for understanding perspectives. Most managers will recognise that different initiatives fit into one or other of the boxes. Dow, for example, set out with the initial purpose of simplifying and harvesting from its massive portfolio of patents when it launched its Intellectual Asset Management Programme in 1993. The aims behind Buckman Laboratories' K'Netix system are primarily to capture and share the knowledge of Buckman associates and to better harvest it through client applications. In both organisations there is recognition that knowledge assets are created through new and improved knowledge processes, and that knowledge processes can be improved through the application of new knowledge assets.

Purposes of knowledge management

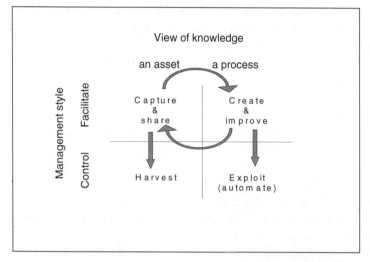

Effective knowledge management involves both facilitation and control. The first supports the creation and capture of new knowledge, while the second enables organisations to benefit from it.

Knowledge process management in a stable environment involves identifying and exploiting tacit processes by making them explicit and placing them on the real shop floor. The more people know the processes the better. Automating tacit knowledge into a process ensures that it is always applied, whether or not employees understand it. IBM calls this 'represented' knowledge. The assembly lines of the last century are the most obvious examples of such knowledge management. One reason why Ford's assembly lines were so successful was that the knowledge needed to meet America's growing demand for Model T cars was built into the assembly lines. This overcame the lack of skills in the available workforce. Expanding production required more capital machinery containing the represented knowledge. The lack of knowledge in new employees was not a problem.

There are many processes which require absolute standards of reliability that are best served by making them explicit. Nearly all the nuclear power station accidents have been due to human error. At both Chernobyl and Three-Mile Island, operatives disregarded or over-rode automated controls, trusting unwisely in their tacit knowledge. Their unmanaged virtual shop floor activities put millions of lives at risk. In Britain, recent train accidents caused when trains under the control of drivers passed red lights, have led to demands for automated systems that ensure trains stop.

In practice no organisation has a single purpose or is likely to remain constantly focused on a single purpose. At Dow, the initial focus on harvesting grew to include capturing, sharing and exploiting. The initial aim of Sun Systems' SunTAN (Training Access Network) in 1996 was to cut the cost of training its sales professionals, but SunTAN soon became a vital integrative sales support system connecting and informing Sun resellers. The training and education purpose gave way to a wider knowledge sharing and development role.

Knowledge management efforts can also be defeated by overly ambitious objectives. Potential knowledge managers have to be realistic in assessing both the management style and definition of knowledge. A strategy that focuses entirely on facilitating creative knowledge processes or depends on managers as facilitators will not succeed in corporations where knowledge is viewed primarily as an asset and where managers serve as controllers. When Niall Hayes and Geoff Walsham looked at the electronic communities of sales practitioners in Compound UK, they found communities that initially were set up to facilitate the creation and sharing of knowledge within the sales force. However, managers came to recognise that the system also could serve as a tool to monitor and control individual performance. As sales reps learned how their participation in the communities was being used to control them, the sales force lost confidence in them as safe environments for creating and sharing knowledge. They stopped participating. Ultimately, management efforts to increase the usefulness of the communities turned facilitation into direct management control.

The electronic communities at Compound UK degenerated into management tools for the exploitation of knowledge processes.

In an issue of *Knowledge Management* magazine, a feature on knowledge engineering revealed the editors' strong belief in managers as controllers[1].

> 'To be relevant KM has to tell workers what to do each day – what to do the same and what to do differently. By applying knowledge, workers add their own contribution to it.'

It is a vision of organisations where managers manage and workers work. Managers possess the knowledge and workers simply respond to it or, at best, contribute at the edges. The point is not to condemn such managerial perspectives, which may apply in some industries and in some situations, but to warn that knowledge work takes place in many real and different organisational contexts that need to be understood if it is to be managed effectively.

The form knowledge management takes in an organisation sends a strong message to managers and workers alike about the relative worth and nature of their contributions. At Compound UK, for example, too little attention was paid either to the emotional needs or to the knowledge possessed by individual sales reps and the initiative failed. The original notion of a forum where reps could freely share their knowledge was incompatible with their managers' attempts to use the forum to monitor and control.

Means

Some of the greatest confusion in knowledge management concerns its means. How do we do it? For most of us, the first contact with knowledge management is associated with new information and communications technology applications. This sometimes creates the impression that knowledge management is

---

[1] The editors, 'K-map part 4: process: putting it into practice', *Knowledge Management*, vol. 2.1, January 1999.

purely an application of technology. It is not. Knowledge management depends on social enablers.

If only it were just a technology problem...

Numerous adverts emphasise technological solutions to knowledge management problems. The following, for example, views the minds of employees as places of concealment. The notion of knowledge management as people management is completely absent.

<u>We make the hidden obvious.</u>

There's a ton of knowledge buried in your business. Concealed in documents. Hidden in Websites. Trapped in the minds of employees.

But what good is that knowledge if no one can get to it?

At [company name], *we provide the only enterprise document and knowledge management software with the power to find, apply and re-use your company's collective expertise. By revealing and maximising what you already know, your company becomes more innovative. More responsive to change. And, ultimately, more competitive.*

*To make your company's hidden strengths more obvious call 1-888-****** or visit our Website at www*****

Practically all corporations which have invested seriously in information and communications technology possess technically efficient systems. Unfortunately, technical capacities do not necessarily result in satisfactory organisational performance. The means of managing knowledge are social practices. In chapter three, we looked at the knowledge processes of the virtual shop floor and saw how they are connected to the performance of real shop floor activities. As discussed, there are four main elements in the knowledge process:

1. Finding out
2. Sharing
3. Memorising
4. Applying.

The knowledge process cycle in organisations

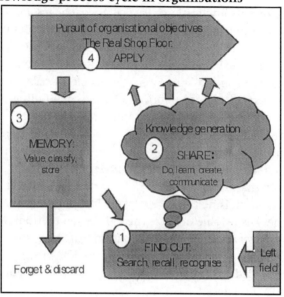

1. The means of finding out knowledge

Usable knowledge comes from experience and memory. The Web and intranets have enormously expanded our capacity to find things out by making it possible to search, filter and access information more rapidly and widely. Finding out may involve responding to identified information needs or known knowledge gaps, or it may be a simple case of satisfying curiosity. At some stage it becomes a defined activity requiring clear understanding of the nature of the search and its parameters. The speed and comprehensiveness of Web and intranet searches contribute to the efficiency of searching and recalling, though raising the likelihood of information overload. Knowledge managers need to ensure that the capacity of technology to speed searching does not blind them to the requirements of the human process of digesting search results.

Recognition is the key element in finding things out. Explicit knowledge usually does not relate precisely to the question at hand. However cleverly a search engine has found a crucial document, it takes the human capacities of the searcher to explore and interpret its implications. Particular challenges are presented by new tacit knowledge, which is likely to go unannounced and may go unnoticed even by its possessors. They may use it unknowingly or fail to see its wider potential. The knowledge management challenge is to find a way to enable people to recognise it and make it explicit. Means include formal de-briefings, project histories and the sponsorship of communities of practice.

At Anglian Water, for example, the withdrawal of direct government control of water companies (the 'golden share') signaled a need to examine competitive capacities. Management discovered that the first stage in managing knowledge at Anglian would involve raising the respect of engineers and technicians for what they were able to do. There is a quote from Marshall McLuhan, '*I'm not sure who discovered water, but I'm certain it wasn't a fish.*' Like many others with specialised craft knowledge, Anglian's people needed to '*step outside themselves*' to recognise their knowledge for what it was.

An often-quoted knowledge management example is Xerox's Eureka system for sharing insights amongst copier repair technicians. Perhaps its most important element is not that it makes explicit and shares the innovations of repairmen, but that it teaches individual repairmen to believe that what they know and do is valuable. Without the confidence that comes from seeing colleagues rewarded for sharing, the Xerox repairmen would be unlikely to risk making their tacit knowledge explicit.

There is no 'best way' to find things out, but there are ways that organisations can become better at it. Good information system design is an essential first step. If people are comfortable with their corporate system they are more likely to use it. It is not enough to merely be efficient at gathering information. Systems that become enormous hoards of information do not work. At Nortel Networks, the enormity of its 1.5 million page intranet was defeating its purpose. Employees demanded a smaller and more accessible intranet. Some undoubtedly valuable information was lost, but Nortel Networks' management believes that the more intensive getting of knowledge from the smaller system justifies their approach.

Equally, there needs to be an approach to managing people that rewards curiosity. Most organisational knowledge-getting is crippled by 'need-to-know' attitudes. How can any searcher know what she needs to know until she finds it? More than that, how can an organisation hope to share knowledge effectively when the culture, structure and job descriptions combine to confine people into widely understood 'need-to-know' knowledge limits? Albert Einstein was a lowly Swiss civil servant, not a physicist. When IBM's John Blackwell appraises his team of consultants he asks them to explain how they have gone about looking for new knowledge and how they have helped others do so. His purpose is not to measure knowledge-getting scientifically, but to embed in them a belief in the value of searching.

2. The means of sharing knowledge

Knowledge generation is also a process of sharing. The blend of doing, learning, communicating and creating that accompanies the operation of the real shop floor is the least understood component of the virtual shop floor, because it is so deeply integrated into the activity of the real one. The easy and fatal mistake is to assume that the visible and manageable information and communication system set up to support knowledge sharing is the one that is being used. However, as Sue Honore's story suggested in chapter two, the more people attach significance to shared knowledge, the more obvious is the extent of effort made to share it. She filtered her e-mail aggressively to force senders to make it more clear to her which messages most deserved her attention.

The trick with managing knowledge sharing is to understand that it is already happening and to find out how it is happening.

Only then can management practices start to support it or help to migrate practices into more efficient electronic forms. Too often, wishful thinking leads managers to assume that their flash intranet will be used, simply because it would be so efficient if it were used. Corporate intranets are clogged with dead conference rooms last used as long as three or four years ago and none containing more than a handful of messages.

At a major global telecommunications company, they developed a new systems tool in 1998 to support virtual team creation through a skills, interests and experience profile database. Managers were proud of the initiative and presented it at a benchmarking forum early the following year. It emerged during discussions that virtual teams in the corporation were still being set up the old way, through personal networks. As one of the project sponsors explained, *'You know some people you trust and they know some more.'* The project manager acknowledged that her own profile was not in the database, because she *'was not used to working that way yet.'*

Geoff Smith, knowledge transformation manager at Cap Gemini UK, argues that the usage of systems depends on how well the systems support people in achieving their business purposes. He warns that people, departments and divisions in organisations will be at different levels of what Cap Gemini has termed *'knowledge maturity.'* This means that overall strategies for sharing will always depend on close understanding of local situations in their implementation. The willingness of one part of the organisation to share must be matched by the other part's willingness to receive, and they both have to agree on the means of sharing.

Knowledge audits and maps can be excellent ways of tracking the potential for sharing practices in an organisation. A good map will set out what is known and where it is located in the organisation. An excellent map will give insights into the routes along which it is shared. They are bridges between tacit and explicit knowledge by enabling knowledge seekers to make connections. In some organisations the metaphor of a 'knowledge market' is used. The map helps connect supply with demand.

Tips on building a knowledge map

The key to knowledge mapping is to think of them as real maps. They help people plan journeys by identifying key locations and possible routes. They need to show only locations and routes that are up-to-date and usable. Never set out to map all the knowledge in an organisation, but only what is relevant to the purpose of the map.

- Establish the focus of the map around a clearly defined topic such as a major market, a technology or an event. For example, South American markets, laser print technology and Y2K have all inspired knowledge maps.
- Align the purpose of the map with strategic objectives. If the strategic objectives are not clear, the map may become too large and difficult to use. Employees need to understand why it is worth contributing to and using. The South American market map was concerned·with supporting entry into the continent by a new competitor.
- Think of the map as a guide to finding knowledge and not as a repository. Most knowledge is tacit. The map should not just be a record of explicit knowledge, which ought to be already accessible through the corporate information system. Like all maps, it is only a guide which helps the user decide on a preferred route from a range of choices.
- Hold people responsible for creating and maintaining visible linkages. Like any dated map, users will stop using it as soon as it helps them to get lost.
- Use linkages to identify possessors of knowledge, updated documents and appropriate databases. The map should show the most important locations of knowledge.
- Frame entries onto the map by type. Entries are grouped into sections such as documentation, internal contacts, external contacts and related knowledge.

> • Have a single entry point to the map, where there is a core document to explain its purpose and architecture and to define its limits. If the map is on a corporate intranet, this might be the homepage.

Despite the importance of the IT system in supporting sharing, the extent of sharing is ruled by social considerations more than technical ones. In most corporate environments, knowledge is power. It is only shared with trusted colleagues via trusted routes. Managers can only begin to facilitate changes in knowledge process by understanding and building on the current extent and modes of sharing.

3. The means of memorising knowledge

Knowledge is memorised through the corporate information systems. Ideally, they will be the official corporate networks like Buckman's K'Netix or Andersen Consulting's Knowledge Xchange, but some of the largest corporations in the world still operate with multiple separate unconnected databases and an enormous amount of additional knowledge still sits in folders, filing cabinets and briefcases.

The quality of information system technology is such that corporate memory can be linked to the operation of the real shop floor in a way that does not create additional pressures on employees, but it often does. At SG Chemical, despite the best efforts of a dedicated team of information managers to rescue a failing system, employees knew that their most senior managers begrudged the time and effort of entering information into the system[2]. It was an unwelcome extra duty that distracted from operational duties. The intranet remained external and additional to the virtual and real shop floor activities it was supposed to support.

---

[2] The story of SG Chemical's system was written up by myself and John Kawalek, and published as 'Trouble on the virtual shop floor' in *Knowledge Directions*, vol. 1, 1999.

The worst examples of organisational memorisation do not just become irrelevant, they do actual damage through the excessive demands they make on employees.

The university sector in Great Britain supplies an excellent illustration. Separate records must be kept on every aspect of every course's operation as part of the Quality Assurance Audit (QAA) that all university subject areas must go through to maintain their status. These records are in addition to the records kept as part of the management of the student experience. At practically every British university, QAA records are in paper format in boxes in special rooms and little has been done to integrate administrative and QAA record-keeping. There are examples of poor scores on quality audits where the poor quality of the records made it impossible for the quality of the teaching to be accurately assessed. Worst of all, the memorisation for QAA is entirely isolated. It informs no other university function.

But it does not have to be that way. At Hewlett-Packard, when sales representatives are entering orders into the system, the order becomes part of corporate memory as well as the front page of the order file. Later entries from other people involved in meeting the order enrich the memory file and drive forward the process of meeting the order.

The order procedure lies at the heart of Hewlett-Packard's real shop floor operations. Integrating the procedure into memory in this way means that important knowledge processes of the virtual shop floor are made visible without laying on employees the requirement to make extra records.

During a conversation at the first meeting of the Institute for Knowledge Management in New York early in 1999, IBM's John Blackwell described the ideal information system as one where the capture of information for memory is *'almost a happy accident as people do what they are supposed to do, making things and making sales. It shouldn't get in the way!'* The Hewlett-Packard system shows just such an approach, while the British university experience is an example of the exact opposite. As such it is resented as a task that is additional to existing workloads.

Electronic point of sale (EPOS) systems supply some of the best examples of successfully linked operation and memory systems being used to generate explicit knowledge that drives management decision-making. Argos has employed an EPOS system for years to inform and drive its just-in-time logistics approach to ordering from suppliers and to stocking its catalogue outlets. Greenall's Pubs and Restaurants, a division of Greenall PLC, has connected the tills of its 500 outlets and uses the information to monitor sales generally, but also to identify unusual sales patterns in individual outlets. These may suggest failings by managers of pubs, but can also indicate where tacit knowledge is located, that Greenall's could make available throughout the chain.

One of the quickest ways to evaluate knowledge management performance is to test an organisation via its homepages on the Internet. The *New York Times* did just that in 1998 soon after IMS Health, the main source of pharmaceutical sector information, was floated. The *Times* reporter sought answers to basic questions about best-selling prescription drugs and global pharmaceutical firms. To the deep embarrassment of IMS, the reporter was not able to find the answers. No one is suggesting that IMS did not know about Glaxo or Prozac, but where was the information kept? Alas for IMS, not where the reporter could find it. Not only was IMS Health not using its site to manage its current knowledge, it created a wrong impression that it lacked such knowledge.

A visit to National Semiconductor's site would reveal a different approach reflecting how its homepages are connected to its operational activities. This enables National Semiconductor to deliver the most up-to-date information to customers and potential customers, but more than that, it enables the corporation to harvest new information from visitors for the purposes of demand forecasting. It is considered a key factor in National Semiconductor's ability to bring new products to market at half the industry average.

4. *The means of applying knowledge*
The application of knowledge should be the main driver for the whole knowledge management exercise. The emphasis

throughout this book has been on the integration of the virtual and real shop floors to achieve business objectives. Knowledge and information processes that are not integrated with operational processes are additional burdens for knowledge workers.

Obviously, knowledge workers already apply knowledge processes to their real shop floor duties. If the knowledge management system does not support them, then it's being done badly and needs to be reviewed. SG Chemical has visible evidence, in the form of its under-used corporate intranet, that its knowledge management vehicle does not work well. The profitability of SG Chemical suggests that its knowledge processes are in fact working and are integrated with the real shop floor, but they are happening in ways and via media that are hidden from managers. They are not, for the most part, happening on the official corporate intranet. It may be that the SG intranet is badly designed or the support for employee use may be inadequate. In any case, SG Chemicals cannot be said to be managing its knowledge processes. Hewlett-Packard, on the other hand, has clear evidence that its intranet is the main communication channel for its real shop floor operations. As do Buckman and IBM. Extensive and growing use of intranets in these companies is one sign that knowledge management is working for them.

How can we understand why one corporation's information system investments support improved knowledge management, when another's do not? Far too often, management confuses investment in the information system with investment in the knowledge management process. Susan Clarke of the IT strategy group Butler Direct emphasised this when she commented on the implications of knowledge management means unlinked to business purpose:

'Many enterprises mistakenly believe that installing a technical knowledge management solution (e.g. an intranet) will solve their problems. However, unless accompanied by a knowledge management strategy, such implementations will almost inevitably fail to meet high expectations.'

Metrics of knowledge management

Of all the problems that knowledge management faces, the most often raised is the lack of easy to understand metrics of the benefits it brings. Knowledge management cannot be confined in a single department or have its unique contribution separated out from, say, that of the design department or finance. Inevitably managers, who must answer ultimately to shareholders with their profit and loss accounts and balance sheets, are cautious about knowledge management.

Nonetheless, there are a range of ways to measure the impact of a knowledge management programme. One of the key indicators of successful knowledge management at Buckman Laboratories has been the rise in what Robert Buckman calls '*effective engagement time*' as a proportion of total employee time. Effective engagement is time spent satisfying the needs and expectations of customers. In 1994, Buckman estimated that 50% of staff were effectively engaged. In 1998 he estimated that around 75% were so engaged and predicted 80% for the turn of the Millennium. At Buckman there is an explicit and widely understood purpose in its knowledge management.

The Buckman example points both to the need to follow general rules and the need to shape measures to fit the requirements of individual situations. The rules are simple:

1. Identify and prioritise one or two strategic objectives. Vague notions of shared knowledge and best practices are doomed.
2. Fit the programme to the existing social dynamics of the organisation. Don't force new knowledge practices, broaden and deepen existing ones.
3. Make sure top sponsors stay involved. Don't let them break the bottle of champagne unless they plan to travel on the maiden voyage.

Measuring the impact of knowledge management

Business excellence

At Barclays Bank, they have placed knowledge management at the heart of an overall business excellence strategy. Barclays is using the Business Excellence Model to measure performance. All of the enablers have been recast to reflect the focus on knowledge. The first enabler of excellence in leadership, for instance, has been recast as 'How do leaders demonstrate commitment to a culture in which knowledge and organisational learning can be fully exploited in the drive towards business excellence?'

Cap Gemini has followed a similar path, redefining the categories and measures of the Business Excellence Model to reflect its Knowledge Maturity Model. The model is set out in the form of a matrix. Organisations are judged against knowledge capture and conversion performance, and knowledge distribution and take-up, as set out below. Managers can map out where their organisations are with respect to individual functions and for overall processes. For example, it was only in the 1970's that many

Key stages in the Knowledge Maturity Model

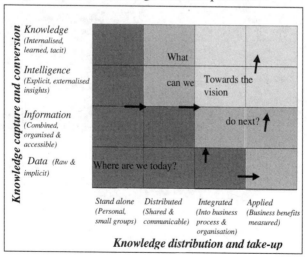

(by permission Cap Gemini Group)

car makers put in place central structures to offer dealerships training in servicing. Before then, expertise was isolated in different dealerships and undistributed across the service network. Today, Ford has gone still further and integrated its dealership network into its overall corporate quality programme.

Geoff Smith at Cap Gemini suggests that it is useful to take a step beyond the Knowledge Maturity Model to assess the overall knowledge perspective of the organisation. It is important to bear in mind that most corporate knowledge management efforts start from a relatively low base. Success will only come in stages and over time. Practically all corporations are now rich in data and information, but few are consistently effective at creating knowledge or at exploiting information as effectively as they might. Practically none are what he calls *'knowledge-driven... where there is total integration between the capabilities of information systems to highlight potential opportunities with the experience and skills of the people.'* For such an organisation, *'by the time the competition has caught up, the organisation will have moved on...'*

Organisational knowledge perspectives

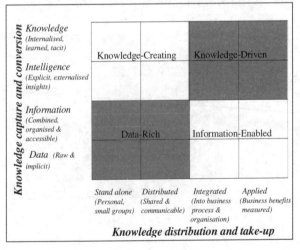

(by permission Cap Gemini Group)

Copyrights and patents

There can be immediate and easily identifiable benefits derived from improved management of explicit knowledge. Both IBM and Dow Chemicals have achieved significant profits from the active management of their stock of copyrights and patents. Andersen, KPMG and other major consultancies use their databases of proposals and reports to inform and improve future proposals and reports, saving time and leveraging quality. Benefits show up in the form of fewer consultant days tied up in proposal preparation and more competitive pricing of tenders.

IBM's first major knowledge management success arose from the decision to manage its patent warehouse commercially, an example of information-enabled asset exploitation. From a position of practically no revenue in 1993, it achieved revenues approaching $9 billion in 1998.

New product and market development

A whole range of development metrics might be used to measure the impact of knowledge management. These include the ratio of new products to total offerings, speed of new product development from initial proposal to market launch and cost of development. Managers at Buckman Laboratories point to a better than 50% improvement in its new product ratio as a key measure of success.

In general, if knowledge management is working well for a corporation, projects should be completed more quickly and with less trouble. One of the main reasons why Britain's flagship departmental retailer, Marks and Spencer, drifted onto the rocks in the late 1990's was its six month cycle of spring and autumn clothing fashions. Nimble new competitors like French Connection change as often as the market requires, so much so that they cannot be said to have seasonal lines at all. At the heart of the Marks and Spencer turn-around strategy is its need to become more responsive to the fickleness of fashion.

Internal benchmarks

Much of knowledge management is about integration across functions that can only be assessed through internal measures. These include usage of and satisfaction with its instruments. This needs to be more in depth than the notorious 'hit rate' measure (the number of times a page is opened). In a way, this is an extension of the initial knowledge map. It helps managers assess if the new routes are being used, and how the flow and location of knowledge is being altered.

All of the most successful knowledge managers regularly review knowledge processes in their organisations. BT has developed a model it calls the 'KM Strategy Lens' which assesses business units in technology, performance, market and culture. BT is looking to include knowledge management issues in individual appraisal as well.

Employee attitudes

A claimed benefit of knowledge management is that it makes it easier and more pleasant for knowledge workers to focus on their jobs. That being so, qualitative measures of employee satisfaction should reflect the improved working environment, and quantitative measures in the form of improved retention rates and recruitment quality.

Knowledge managers should be warned though. Improved attitudes may not happen at once or be shared amongst all staff. In 1994 the human resource department at Blue Cross/Blue Shield, New Jersey, decided to plan and manage its migration from a mainframe into a new client/server system without the support of an uncooperative information systems department[3]. A significant minority of people could not cope with the change. They quit, were released or moved into departments where the mainframe system still operated. Nonetheless, within two years the department's initiative had proved so successful that it was being asked to support the moves of Blue Cross/Blue Shield of Delaware and Connecticut to the new system.

---

[3] Randy Weston, 'HR to IS: resistance is futile', *Computerworld*, 9 December 1996.

Customer satisfaction and loyalty

The ultimate purpose of the virtual shop floor is to enable the real shop floor to be more effective. Thus the most important metric for knowledge management must be its impact on customers. As with employees, a mixture of qualitative and quantitative measures are possible. Corporations should look for greater loyalty from existing customers and increased competitiveness with potential new customers. At Rebus International, when it redesigned its system for tracking help-desk queries, it found that it had made visible the quantity and nature of improvements and fault corrections not just to internal staff but to its customers. The response was overwhelmingly positive. Help-desk support is quicker and more positive because both Rebus' technical people and customers are better informed.

Many knowledge management initiatives lose managerial backing because the metrics of customer satisfaction and loyalty are not always clear-cut. The problem with these metrics is that they are mainly indicative rather than definitive; mainly qualitative rather than quantitative.

They require an imaginative approach to metrics and will not convince those who seek 'hard' financial evidence. IBM's knowledge management guru, Larry Prusak, believes that decision-makers from financial and engineering backgrounds find such measures harder to accept than those from arts and humanities backgrounds. He suggests that this has made life more difficult for knowledge management in the United States where CEOs are drawn predominantly from engineering and finance.

Conclusion – knowing how to manage knowledge

Every organisation is different and interacts with its environment in different ways, but the principles of knowledge management apply to all of them. Organisations need to create, identify, share, apply and remember knowledge in pursuit of organisational objectives in the context of a changeable environment. New knowledge is the factor that enables organisations to align with the environment as it shifts. Organisational knowledge processes must be flexible, because the environment is flexible.

Inflexible knowledge processes lead to a dependence on dated and irrelevant knowledge. A former marketing manager at a British insurance company, who lost his job in 1994, put it this way, *'We spent 200 years serving our market. Even while it was disappearing, we couldn't stop doing things like we always had.'* He described meetings where the emergence of new channels and related developments were usually viewed as *'things to be fought'*, as if the environment could somehow be realigned back to match the company's unchanging perspective.

Above all, knowledge management depends on an appreciation of organisational objectives. Once managers can place corporate knowledge processes within a strategic framework, defining practices and applying metrics becomes possible. Just as vaguely focused quality initiatives were utterly transcended by tightly defined and measured Total Quality Management, so the fuzzy and uncertain visions of knowledge-based, information-rich organisations will be left behind as genuine applications of knowledge management prove their worth.

8

Conclusions – the future of knowledge management

Introduction

Perhaps the most satisfying outcome of writing *From Know-How to Knowledge* has been the way it has helped to clarify my own appreciation of knowledge management as a logical next step in the developing practice of corporate management. During my time as a manager, consultant and academic, I have read many management gurus. The stream of *essential* management solutions that has characterised the current business era made me cautious of knowledge management. Does the world really need another *'cure'* for the problems of management?

But, knowledge management *is* different. It offers no standard recipe that has to be followed. Its basic premise is that organisations need to manage knowledge better, but they need to do it their own way. *From Know-How to Knowledge* is not an instructional manual. It describes tools and discusses methods of managing knowledge, but how you use them will be shaped by the knowledge processes and the knowledge needs of your particular organisation.

Throughout our managerial lives, we approach problems cautiously. We *'stick to the knitting'* to avoid situations that require new thinking, and we '*don't fix it if it ain't broke*'. In general, when managers manage, they start by making sure things are being done according to the set procedures and in line with past history. If that brings success, they see no further need for action but, if it fails, managers start to look at the individual components of the process – how can they be improved? It is only when all else fails that the ultimate purpose of the process comes into question.

In the coming decade, knowledge management will become a central aspect of organisational development because it matches the way the business environment is changing. Markets are demanding increasingly individualistic and higher quality supply and the capacities of firms to satisfy demand are rising in response. Competition is forcing firms to seek out differences that cannot be imitated. Technology can always be matched by determined competitors. Natural resources can be purchased. Information can be acquired. Know-how can be copied or bypassed. Ultimately, the only truly defensible corporate competitive advantage is the unique capacity of its people to engage in knowledge work. All else has failed.

Key lessons

The key lessons from the emergence of knowledge management are simple, and owe more to common sense than deep philosophical musings on the meaning and nature of management. Knowledge management is not rocket science.

First: Knowledge processes inform *all* our 'real' corporate processes. All the activities involved in manufacturing, distributing, servicing and generally doing whatever our markets require, are enabled and accompanied by the thinking, learning, informing, communicating, discovering and creating of the virtual shop floor. The increasing capacity of organisations to undertake real shop floor activities efficiently is an inevitable result of the way information technology improvements and related forces have simplified the business environment and made the real shop floor's workings more visible.

In order to stay competitive, corporations need to start with the understanding that the advantages they achieve over competitors can be seen and copied. Ultimately, their success depends on the knowledge dynamics of the virtual shop floor, because that is where the capacity to create new competitive advantages lies.

Second: The value of information is determined by its recipients and not by its senders. Information management is only effective when it is aligned with corporate knowledge processes. If information does not contribute to the understanding and decision-making of those who receive it, then it is wasting their time.

The fundamental reason why so many information systems perform badly is that they are what marketers used to call product-led developments, rather than market-led ones. Assumptions are made about information content and communication channels without adequate regard for the needs of the knowledge workers and processes that they are supposed to serve. Thus, improvements in information and communications technology require deeper corporate understanding and management of knowledge processes to give them purpose.

Third: When information is no longer scarce, it is the capacity of knowledge workers to use it that becomes the process bottleneck. Today, e-mail, intranets and the Internet all ensure that knowledge workers have access to far more information than they can digest. It consumes their time and their attention. In many ways, the very name 'knowledge management' is unhelpful and misleading, because it reduces knowledge from a process to a thing.

But knowledge management is ultimately about improving the processes of learning, creating and sharing meaning in organisations. The bottleneck needs to be removed in a way that enhances corporate capacities to benefit from knowledge processes. Many of the problems caused by poor knowledge management are due to practices that ease the bottleneck but damage the knowledge

processes. Deleting the whole in-box may be emotionally satisfying, but it is not a solution.

Fourth: As information about the business environment becomes
more accessible, more and more market participants are
managing knowledge to their advantage. When competitors,
customers and suppliers are able to use knowledge processes more
effectively it becomes a defensive necessity that corporations do it
as well. Otherwise they are placed at too great a disadvantage.

The challenges and opportunities that the environment throws
up are too many and too varied for organisations to know how to
respond to all of them. They do need to have the capacity to understand the challenges so that they can learn how to respond to
them. It will become increasingly clear over time that success
depends on how organisations respond mentally and emotionally
to environmental changes. At the very least, knowledge
management offers the possibility of guiding our organisations
towards an improved and managed capacity to do that.

Fifth: The common denominator for the different types of
knowledge is their organisational purpose. Knowledge
management, like all other forms of management, needs to be
framed by a strategic appreciation of the nature of the knowledge
challenge.

Organisations that become too focused on managing
knowledge as an asset are neglecting the connection between the
changing environment and their strategic focus. As the
environment shifts, so the required knowledge alters. Effective
knowledge management focuses on knowledge processes and the
flow of knowledge, because without the inflow of new knowledge,
the pool of relevant knowledge will one day dry up.

The future

This book is a guide, so it must address the future of knowledge
management as well as its present practice. Chapter one started by
posing the question, '*Do the groaning shelves of the airport bookstores*

really need another new business fad?' Is it a passing craze? Almost certainly, yes, in the sense that the term *knowledge management* will be replaced by another. What is not a fad is the focus of knowledge management. Managers will concern themselves more and more with the processes of knowledge as time goes on, because they must.

What they will call it is anyone's guess. Managers used to manage *hands*, and hands supplied their labour. The term knowledge management is an improvement, because hands have become *brains* and labour has given way to knowledge. It is not ultimately enough, though. Our participation in knowledge processes is social. We share and we withhold what we know according to our personal perspectives. There is probably a new term already lining up to replace knowledge management. What will *not* be replaced are its principles and tools.

All the available evidence suggests that knowledge management will become a progressively more important aspect of organisational performance for the foreseeable future. Major players like IBM and Microsoft have made it the centre-piece of their vision for the twenty-first century.

Here is IBM's Lou Gerstner:

'We've been re-engineering IBM from top to bottom with one goal: to foster a high performance culture and turn IBM into the world's premier knowledge management company.'

...and Microsoft's Bill Gates:

'Any company wishing to compete in the Digital Age faces the challenge of gathering and utilising their corporate knowledge more effectively than their competitors. This will be fundamental to the way many organisations succeed in business in the early twenty-first century. Because of this, knowledge management is a key focus for the Digital Nervous System, Microsoft's defining vision for how businesses can use information technology to create sustainable competitive advantage in the new Digital Economy.'

Sales revenue is becoming more dependent on knowledge and less dependent on tangible assets. The rise in productivity that has characterised the last twenty-five years has not been accompanied by an equivalent rise in capital investment. It has been due to a more intelligent use of capital. At IBM, for example, desk-top computers have given way to lap-tops that can be plugged into systems wherever there is a telephone line. The SunRay from Sun Systems is simply a powerful screen that draws all its capabilities from whatever server it is connected to. Everywhere hot desk office bases accommodate more employees in smaller sites. These are developments that aim to enable people to employ their knowledge more creatively and productively as the environment shifts and their knowledge changes.

Corporations over-dependent on expensive and inflexible tangible assets will be unable to respond to shifts in their business environment, and it will be due to management mistakes. Warehouses full of parts are insurance against the failure to manage supply processes well enough. Quality assurance recalls are expensive means of compensating for process weaknesses. The very success of initiatives such as just-in-time and Total Quality arise from more effective knowledge processes.

With the formal acknowledgement of knowledge management, corporations are recognising the common thread that runs through the history of management development; from suggestion boxes through quality circles and on to learning organisations, business process engineering and the present. What connects them all is that they are based on developing, capturing and employing the good will and knowledge of the people associated with the organisation to stay aligned with their business environment.

Journey's end?

The journey from know-how to knowledge management has no end. It is a race with no rules. Pity the poor competitor, having navigated her way to the front of the field only to find that some of the competitors she passed on the way were craftily climbing onto horses or getting into cars, while others were opening up a completely different race track. Yet, that is the knowledge manager's lot. If you have made the journey from know-how to knowledge, then you understand already. You have not reached its end, you have reached its beginning...

Further reading

The range of literature on knowledge management is growing in leaps and bounds, so this can only be a rough, and quite personal, guide. Readers will develop their own focus very quickly.

Ikujiro Nonaka and Hirotaka Takeuchi, *The Knowledge-creating Company*, Oxford University Press, 1995. Start with the most inspired. Certainly the Japanese economy has gone off the boil, leaving some of the authors' notions of the 'Japanese-ness' of knowledge management looking thin, but it is a powerful discussion of the philosophical bases and an excellent read.

T. H. Davenport and L. Prusak, *Working Knowledge*, Harvard Business School Press, 1998. This is the best American knowledge management book targeted at practitioners. It is weak in the way it avoids explaining exactly what the authors mean by knowledge, but it is rich in examples of its practice and does explore many of the issues in great depth. Above all, they write well.

Clayton Christiansen, *The Innovator's Dilemma*, Harvard Business School, 1997. This is another well-written story. It is not directly about knowledge management, but focuses on how and why excellently managed companies so often fail. It will be difficult not to see why knowledge management is so important after reading Christiansen.

Marshall McLuhan, *Understanding Media*, McGraw-Hill, New York, 1964. Marshall McLuhan was one of the gurus of the 1960's. This is his classic. In it, he predicts the current business environment with uncanny accuracy. His insight into how information and communications technology affects social organisations and individuals is what should interest the knowledge manager.

Unlike the other writers, he can be difficult to read, but his insights are astonishing. You only need to read the first two and final chapters to get the heart of his message.

Thomas Stewart, *Intellectual Capital*, Nicholas Brealey, London, 1997. Stewart is an editor of *Fortune* magazine and it shows in this book in the way he smoothly constructs a description that concentrates on knowledge the asset, rather than knowledge processes. That is its great limitation. Readers will be interested in his attempt to find accountancy-based metrics of the asset value of intellectual capital. If this is the only KM book you can read, don't read it, but if you can read more widely, it offers some real insights from an accountancy perspective.

Michael J. Hammer and James Champy, *Reengineering the Corporation*, Nicholas Brealey, London, 1993. Hammer and Champy comprehensively missed the importance of knowledge and knowledge processes. More than that they said far too little about the difference between efficiency and effectiveness. Nonetheless, to readers with open minds and an appreciation of these issues, BPR offers some powerful tools, however flawed the authors' initial premise.

Oliver Sachs, *The Man Who Mistook his Wife for a Hat*, Picador, 1983. You will never read a better exploration of the nature of the human mind and the different ways that people experience the world and possess knowledge. Do not expect an obvious connection with business or knowledge management, but it is there if you look.

Wendi Bukowitz and Ruth Williams, *The Knowledge Management Fieldbook*, Prentice Hall, 1999. This is a book which starts by dismissing the concepts and theories of knowledge management as essentially irrelevant to its implementation. It sets out to deliver a practical how-to-do-it in great detail. I dislike the approach intensely, because I do not think many successful knowledge management initiatives are likely to be guided by it. Nonetheless, it may appeal to some readers. The authors are practising consultants and write well, though their approach, which involves keeping scores as you go, is difficult to read except in short stages.

Others to read

There are many more interesting books and articles that you could read. The following list contains further interesting material.

Arthur Battram, *Navigating Complexity,* Industrial Society, London, 1998. The first half is an excellent light introduction to the environment that has made knowledge management so necessary. It makes clear the connection between management practice and complexity theory.

Jos Benders, Job de Haan and David Bennet (eds), *The Symbiosis of Work and Technology,* Taylor & Francis, London, 1995. A set of well thought out academic articles on knowledge management practices.

Marc Eisenstadt and Tom Vincent, *The Knowledge Web: Learning and Collaborating on the Net,* Kogan Page, London, 1998. Already slightly dated as e-commerce gathers pace, but helps explain how technology implementations and business structures influence each other.

Roy Jacques, *Manufacturing the Employee*, Sage, London, 1996. An excellent exploration of how management has developed towards knowledge management. The way he draws out the similarities between today and 100 years ago is remarkable. No practical tools in it, but full of provoking arguments that will help you ground your understanding of knowledge management in the context of the historical development of management thinking.